Praise for *Satipaṭṭhāna Meditation: A Practice Guide*

This is a pearl of a book.  it to the author's previous two s{ ... }ression is that of having left the { ... } entered the meditation hall, whe{ ... } teacher is offering Dhamma refle{...}, illuminating the practice of *satipaṭṭhāna* with a fertile and colourful lucidity, free of footnotes and arcane cross-references. This book is a treasure-house of practical teachings, rendered accessible with a clear and simple eloquence. The author states that his motivation has been to enrich the practice of *satipaṭṭhāna* rather than to compete with other approaches – he has succeeded admirably in this, I feel, and with praiseworthy skill and grace.
– **Ajahn Amaro**

This breathtaking practice guide is brief, and profound! It offers a detailed, engaging, and flexible approach to *satipaṭṭhāna* meditation that can be easily applied both in meditation and in day-to-day activities. The inspired practice suggestions and joyful enquiry that pervade each chapter will draw students, gradually but surely, towards deep liberating insight. *Satipaṭṭhāna Meditation: A Practice Guide* is destined to become an invaluable resource for meditators!
– **Shaila Catherine**, author of *Focused and Fearless: A Meditator's Guide to States of Deep Joy, Calm, and Clarity*

Once more Bhikkhu Anālayo has written a masterpiece that holds within it an accessible and clear guide to developing and applying the teachings held within the *Satipaṭṭhāna-sutta*. Within this book Anālayo explores the subtle nuances of developing mindfulness and how that dedicated cultivation leads to the awakening pointed to in the discourse. This is an indispensable meditative guide for anyone truly seeking to understand and know for themselves the liberating insights offered in the four ways of establishing mindfulness.
– **Christina Feldman**, author of *The Boundless Heart*

Bhikkhu Anālayo presents the Buddha's practical teaching of the path to Nibbāna in one comprehensive whole: the wheel of *satipaṭṭhāna*. He writes for practitioners, and his own practice shines through like a beacon. It makes this a very exciting guide for meditators – the truth of it leaps out at you. Each reader can map out for themselves Bhikkhu Anālayo's clear mandala that draws together the entire body of *satipaṭṭhāna* practice. In his simplification the lines of Dharma principle are clear, yet none of the richness and potential is lost. Indeed, as you take in what he is saying, more and more significance dawns.

– **Kamalashila**, author of *Buddhist Meditation: Tranquillity, Imagination and Insight*

SATIPAṬṬHĀNA MEDITATION: A PRACTICE GUIDE

SATIPAṬṬHĀNA MEDITATION: A PRACTICE GUIDE

Bhikkhu Anālayo

Windhorse Publications

Windhorse Publications
info@windhorsepublications.com
windhorsepublications.com

The index was not compiled by the author.

Drawings by Anna Oneglia (www.annaoneglia.com)
Cover design by Dhammarati
Typesetting and layout by Ruth Rudd
Printed by Bell & Bain Ltd, Glasgow

British Library Cataloguing in Publication Data:
A catalogue record for this book is available from
the British Library.

ISBN: 978-1-911407-10-2

CONTENTS

ABOUT THE AUTHOR

Born in 1962 in Germany, Bhikkhu Anālayo was ordained in 1995 in Sri Lanka, and completed a PhD on the *Satipaṭṭhāna-sutta* at the University of Peradeniya, Sri Lanka, in 2000 – published in 2003 by Windhorse Publications under the title *Satipaṭṭhāna, The Direct Path to Realization*.

Anālayo is a professor of Buddhist Studies; his main research area is early Buddhism and in particular the topics of the Chinese *Āgama*s, meditation, and women in Buddhism. Besides his academic pursuits, he regularly teaches meditation. He presently resides at the Barre Center for Buddhist Studies in Massachusetts, where he spends most of his time in silent retreat.

ACKNOWLEDGEMENT AND DEDICATION

I am indebted to Irene Bumbacher, Shaila Catherine, Bhikkhunī Dhammadinnā, Ann Dillon, Linda Grace, Robert Grosch, Hedwig Kren, Yuka Nakamura, and Matt Weingast for commenting on a draft version of this book, and to the staff and supporters of the Barre Center for Buddhist Studies for providing me with the facilities needed to do my practice and writing.

I would like to dedicate this book to the memory of Bhikkhu Katukurunde Ñāṇananda (1940–2018) in gratitude for guidance and inspiration in exploring deep passages among the early discourses from a practice-related perspective.

PUBLISHER'S ACKNOWLEDGEMENTS

Windhorse Publications wishes to gratefully acknowledge a grant from the Triratna European Chairs' Assembly Fund and the Future Dharma Fund towards the production of this book.

We also wish to acknowledge and thank the individual donors who gave to the book's production via our "Sponsor-a-book" campaign.

FOREWORD BY JOSEPH GOLDSTEIN

Bhikkhu Anālayo's first book, *Satipaṭṭhāna, The Direct Path to Realization*, was a seminal work, bridging the divide between rigorous scholarship and meditative understanding and practice. Following in the tradition of great scholar-practitioners, Anālayo illuminated the profound details of the *Satipaṭṭhāna-sutta*, which inspired my own interest in further exploring this pivotal discourse. Meeting Anālayo in person, and later teaching a retreat with him at the Insight Meditation Society, confirmed my initial enthusiasm for what he was offering to Western Dharma practitioners. His remarkable breadth of knowledge and depth of practice have elucidated with great clarity the liberation teachings of the Buddha.

In this current volume, *Satipaṭṭhāna Meditation: A Practice Guide*, Anālayo moves from a more scholarly approach to an eminently pragmatic discussion of how to put these teachings into practice. Although his comparative study of both the Pāli and the Chinese versions of the text informs this work, it is the clear expression of a graduated path of practice that makes it so compellingly helpful. Anālayo has developed a simple and straightforward map of practice instructions encompassing all four *satipaṭṭhāna*s – the body, feelings, mind, and dharmas (the hindrances and awakening factors) – that build upon one another in a coherent and comprehensive path leading to the final goal.

One of the great joys of reading this book is Anālayo's creativity in presenting the teachings of early Buddhism in a way that emphasizes their practical application. To name just a few of the very many examples of this, in the opening chapter there is a clear explanation of what mindfulness actually is, its relation both to memory and to concepts, the feminine nature of its open receptivity and soft alertness (the Pāli word *sati* is feminine), and the fundamental importance of embodied awareness. Given the current widespread popularity of mindfulness, exploring the nuances of what the term means offers us the possibility of greater depth in its cultivation.

There are also detailed descriptions of various death contemplations that give a vivid immediacy to these practices. Anālayo comments that "if I were asked to recommend just one single meditation practice, I would probably opt for recollection of death. This is because of its transformative power."

And in discussing mindfulness of feelings, he does not simply suggest noticing whether they are pleasant, unpleasant, or neutral, but understanding "the way feelings impact the mind". In like manner, Anālayo proceeds through mindfulness of mind and of dharmas, detailing ways of practice that illuminate the conditioned, impermanent nature of all aspects of our experience. These insights culminate in a simple but profound progression from seclusion (from the hindrances) and dispassion through cessation and letting go, leading directly to Nibbāna, the highest peace.

An unusual aspect of Anālayo's work is the combination of precision and openness, highlighting the specificity of particular practices and, at the same time, recognizing that there are many different meditative techniques and approaches. Anālayo continually reminds us to test all the suggestions and to see what works best for each one of us, so that we may all, in the words of the *Satipaṭṭhāna-sutta*, "dwell independently without clinging to anything in the world".

Joseph Goldstein

When based on virtue and established in virtue you thus cultivate these four *satipaṭṭhāna*s, then you can expect growth in wholesome states to come to you, be it day or night, and no decline (SN 47.15).

INTRODUCTION

This is my third book on the topic of *satipaṭṭhāna* meditation. The first book, *Satipaṭṭhāna, The Direct Path to Realization* (2003), was an attempt to survey and collect relevant material for an understanding of the *Satipaṭṭhāna-sutta*. It could be compared to building the foundation for the construction of a house. At that time I tried to gain a better understanding of various details. However, in one way or another, I was still missing the overall picture. It was, after all, just a foundation.

The second book, *Perspectives on Satipaṭṭhāna* (2013), published ten years later, built on that foundation. It could be compared to the walls of the house. By studying the Chinese parallels to the *Satipaṭṭhāna-sutta*, I was able to identify those contemplations that form the common core of this discourse in its various versions. This enabled me to get a better sense of the overall picture of what *satipaṭṭhāna* is all about.

With the present book I return to the Pāli version of the *Satipaṭṭhāna-sutta*. My exploration is entirely dedicated to the actual practice of *satipaṭṭhāna*, informed by the previously gathered details and overall picture as it emerges from a study of relevant material in the early discourses. In terms of my simile of the house, what I now present is the roof of the house – its pinnacle. Of the three books, the present one is also the one most directly aimed at practitioners. I am dispensing with footnotes entirely, as well as with references to studies by others. I use in-line quotation to refer to relevant passages from the Pāli discourses and to my own works by way of date of publication and page to enable readers to follow up particular points of interest. To facilitate tracing the relevant passage from a Pāli discourse, a list of quotes at the end of the book gives cross-references to the relevant page in the standard English translations. For marking supplementations in quotes from my own translation of the *Satipaṭṭhāna-sutta*, I employ italics, similar to the procedure I adopted in other recent publications (Anālayo 2016 and 2017c). In translated passages I replace references to a *bhikkhu* with "one", in order to make it clear that the instructions are not meant for male monastics only.

My overall concern in the following pages is to provide suggestions and inspiration for actual meditation practice. The book comes with audio files that offer meditation instructions, which can be freely downloaded from the publisher's website at https://www.windhorsepublications.com/satipatthana-meditation-audio/. For each of the seven contemplations covered in this book there are audio recordings with guided meditation instructions that build on each other gradually.

I would recommend using the book and recordings to develop the practice step by step. This could be done, for example, over a period of seven weeks. In the early discourses the number seven functions as a symbol of a complete cycle of time. In preparation for this cycle of self-training, I recommend reading the first two chapters. Following such preparation, perhaps each week it would be possible to find time to study one of the chapters on the seven main contemplations, and during the ensuing days of the week cultivate its actual practice. In this way, alongside whatever other responsibilities we might have, it would be possible to complete a course of self-training within a period of seven weeks.

Following such a course of training, we might then continue letting the practice of all four *satipaṭṭhānas* become more and more an integral part of our life. The basic pattern of mindfulness practice remains throughout: being in the present, knowing what is happening, and proceeding accordingly.

I

MINDFULNESS

An indispensable foundation for any *satipaṭṭhāna* practice is
a clear understanding of what mindfulness actually is. Here
I think it is first of all important to acknowledge that there
are various notions of mindfulness. Diverse understandings
of this quality can be found not only among several Buddhist
traditions, but also among those involved with its clinical
employment. Each of these understandings has its own value
and significance (Anālayo 2017a: 26). In what follows, I will
present my own understanding of one of these constructs of
mindfulness, namely the way *sati* is described and reflected
in the early Buddhist discourses. Throughout this book, I use
"mindfulness" and "awareness" as interchangeable translations
for *sati*.

MINDFULNESS AND MEMORY

The standard definition of mindfulness in the discourses brings
in the topic of memory (Anālayo 2003: 46ff, 2013: 30ff, and
2018b). It states that one who is mindful is able to remember
what has been done or said long ago. At first sight this can
give the impression that mindfulness should be equated
with memory. However, closer reflection shows that such an
equation does not work. The problem is that distractions during
meditation practice often involve some memory of the past. It

is a common experience to sit down with the firm intention to be mindful, only to find that sooner or later the mind has wandered off into some past event. The arising of such episodic memories is clearly a case of loss of mindfulness, even though it involves remembering something that has been done or said long ago.

Mindfulness can also be lost when we imagine something taking place in the future. Although this does not involve remembering what has been done or said long ago, daydreaming about the future still concerns aspects of memory, such as working memory and semantic memory. The experience of such distractions during meditation makes it clear that mindfulness cannot just be a form of memory (Anālayo 2017a: 26ff).

Once it has become clear that such a simple equation does not work, another explanation has to be found for appreciating the relationship between mindfulness and memory. My suggestion here is to understand that relationship as implying that the presence of mindfulness enhances and strengthens memory. Full awareness of the present moment will make it easier to recall later what has happened. Moreover, if the receptive stance of mindfulness is established at the time of recalling, it will be easier to access the required information in the mind. In this way mindfulness can be understood to facilitate the taking in of information to be recalled as well as the subsequent successful recollection of that information.

The need to understand mindfulness and memory as two closely interrelated qualities that at the same time are not identical with each other is of consequence for actual practice. Perhaps the most crucial aspect of mindfulness practice is to stay in the present moment. This is what really counts and why it is so important to distinguish clearly between mindfulness and memory. *Satipaṭṭhāna* meditation is not about remembering something from the past, but about being fully in the present moment.

This vital distinction can to some degree be lost sight of with the understanding of mindfulness in the Theravāda commentarial tradition. The commentaries consider mindfulness to be a mental quality that is invariably wholesome. The discourses, however, clearly recognize that there can be wrong types of mindfulness, *micchā sati* (Anālayo 2003: 52 and 2013: 179). These could hardly be considered wholesome. Yet, a discourse in the *Satipaṭṭhāna-saṃyutta* presents the four *satipaṭṭhānas* as a heap of what is wholesome (SN 47.5; Anālayo 2013: 179). In other words, mindfulness itself is not necessarily wholesome. But when mindfulness is cultivated in the form of the four *satipaṭṭhānas*, then such practice does indeed become something definitely wholesome.

A problem with the commentarial understanding, according to which mindfulness itself is invariably wholesome, is that contemplation of an unwholesome state of mind becomes retrospective. This is because, according to the commentarial understanding, wholesome and unwholesome qualities cannot exist simultaneously in the same state of mind. Therefore it becomes impossible for a type of mindfulness that by definition is wholesome to coexist with an unwholesome mental condition such as lust or anger.

This does not reflect what emerges from the early discourses. The instructions on *satipaṭṭhāna* meditation describe being aware of lust or anger, for example, or of any of the five hindrances at the time when they are present in the mind. From this viewpoint, mindfulness can indeed remain established when an unwholesome mental condition is present. In fact it is precisely when unwholesomeness manifests that mindfulness needs to be present. The wholesome repercussions of *satipaṭṭhāna* thus do not imply that certain mental conditions are excluded from being potential objects of direct observation with mindfulness in the present moment. Instead, the point is only that such contemplation has wholesome repercussions. Such an understanding helps to preserve a key aspect of the early Buddhist conception of mindfulness, which is to be fully aware of what is happening right now.

The type of mindful presence to be cultivated in this way is similar to how we would try to be alert and attentive when something takes place that we later have to remember. When walking a path for the first time with the help of a guide, for example, knowing that the next time we will have to find our way on our own, we will make an effort to notice and clearly remember which turns to take. It is this same effort or "diligence" (my preferred translation for *ātāpī*) that we can bring to anything that happens. Regardless of whether we expect to need to remember later what we did, the task is invariably to be fully present, fully there, and fully aware.

I will come back to the significance of the memory connotation for an appreciation of mindfulness in Chapter 9 on the awakening factors (see below p. 173).

CULTIVATING MINDFULNESS

Another aspect of the early Buddhist conception of *sati* is that mindfulness is a mental quality that we have to bring into being. Mindfulness has to be established; it is not just a quality that is present anyway in any type of experience (Anālayo 2017a: 27f). This marks the difference between mindfulness and consciousness. Consciousness, as one of the five aggregates, is a continuously present process of knowing. This does not mean that consciousness is permanent. It only means that the changing flow of moments of being conscious is continuously present. Without this flow of knowing, we would not be experiencing.

Whether we are mindful of a meditation object or caught up in a dream or fantasy, the flow of consciousness is always there. The same does not apply to mindfulness. In fact the notion that there is a constantly present form of awareness which needs to be recognized and which equals the liberated mind does not square with the early Buddhist understanding of mindfulness (or of consciousness). Apparently the outcome of a complex development with a starting point in a discourse that contrasts the luminous mind to its adventitious defilements (AN 1.6.1; Anālayo 2017b), the resultant notion runs counter to the recurrent emphasis on impermanence in the *Satipaṭṭhāna-sutta*, found in the part of the discourse I like to refer to as the "refrain".

Although mindfulness requires cultivation, being a quality that needs to be established, such cultivation is not a forceful matter. Here it can be useful to take into consideration that the word *sati* in the Pāli language is feminine. My suggestion would be to relate to *sati*, to mindfulness, as a feminine quality. In this way, *sati* can be understood as receptively assimilating with the potential of giving birth to new perspectives.

Right away from the moment of waking up in the morning our good friend *sati* can already be there, as if waiting for us. She is ready to accompany us throughout the rest of the day, encouraging us to stay receptive and open, soft and understanding. She never gets upset when we happen to forget about her. As soon as we remember her, she is right there to be with us again.

Visualizing the practice in terms of a coming back to the presence of a good friend helps to avoid mistaking *sati* for a forceful type of hyper-attentiveness that requires strained effort in order to be maintained. Instead, being in her presence carries the flavours of an open receptivity and a soft alertness to whatever is taking place.

MINDFULNESS AND CONCEPTS

Once established in this way, mindfulness can coexist with the employment of concepts. In fact the instructions in the *Satipaṭṭhāna-sutta*, whose function is precisely to foster the establishing of mindfulness, clearly encourage the wise use of concepts. At times the discourse presents these concepts in quotation marks, making it clear that some form of mental verbalization is meant. I understand this to refer to the input provided by the quality of clearly knowing, *sampajañña*, in relation to what has become evident through well-established mindfulness.

The forward thrust of *satipaṭṭhāna* towards liberation does not require keeping the mind free from concepts. The main task is to cultivate a free mind even in the presence of concepts. The path to such freedom is based on the skilful use of certain concepts, namely those that trigger insight. In other words, our attitude towards concepts and thoughts is best informed by the distinction between unwholesome and wholesome types. Although we need to beware of confusing actual practice with just thinking about the practice, wholesome thoughts and concepts can serve as a tool for progress, and in the form of clearly knowing are an integral dimension of *satipaṭṭhāna* meditation.

The input provided by *sampajañña*, clearly knowing, could be illustrated with the example of yeast, due to which the dough of mindfulness practice can grow into the bread of liberating insight. Without yeast, the dough will result only in flatbread. Yeast on its own, however, will not be nourishing at all. It is when the cultivation of mindfulness comes in combination with the right amount of the yeast of clearly knowing that the tasty and nourishing bread of insight will result.

Regarding the role of concepts, it also needs to be kept in mind that a distinction between concepts and ultimate realities is not found in the early Buddhist discourses. For those who practise according to the methodology of the Theravāda commentarial tradition, this distinction is of considerable importance and has its practical benefits. However, for the type of practice that I present here, it would be helpful to set aside this mode of thinking.

In the early discourses, tranquillity and insight are not distinguished according to whether our meditation object is a concept or (what is considered to be) an ultimate reality. In fact tranquillity and insight are not even set apart as separate meditation practices. Instead, they are complementary qualities of meditative cultivation (Anālayo 2017a: 88ff and 173f). Some practices can emphasize one or the other of these two, and with still others tranquillity and insight can be cultivated in conjunction. The only ultimate reality recognized in early Buddhism is Nibbāna. This is the one experience where concepts indeed do not have a place. For the path leading up to this culmination point in the experience of Nibbāna, however, concepts are useful tools.

The need for concepts is also to some degree implicit in a passage in the *Mahānidāna-sutta*, which describes experience as involving a relationship of reciprocal conditioning between consciousness and name-and-form (DN 15; Anālayo 2015: 107f). Here "name" stands for those mental activities responsible for conceptual designation and "form" for the experience of matter by way of resistance. Both together are known by consciousness. From the viewpoint of early Buddhist epistemology, insight into matter cannot take place without name, without at least a minimal input of concept. Only dead matter impinging on dead matter will be free from concepts. But for us to cultivate insight into the true nature of material phenomena, some form of contact by way of designation is required.

In the case of contemplation of the body as the first *satipaṭṭhāna*, for example, the task is not to break through to an ultimately true experience of the body that leaves behind all concepts. Instead, the task is to see through deluding concepts with the help of wise concepts. This takes place by cultivating clearly knowing in conjunction with mindfulness. In short, not only can early Buddhist mindfulness coexist with the use of concepts, *satipaṭṭhāna* meditation even has to employ concepts in order to lead to liberation.

MINDFULNESS AND RECEPTIVITY

Another significant aspect of mindfulness is what I like to refer to as breadth of mind. With breadth of mind I mean an open-minded and broadly receptive attitude. This type of open receptivity can be illustrated with the help of the cowherd simile found in the *Dvedhāvitakka-sutta* (MN 19). This simile describes a cowherd in ancient India in two situations. In the first situation the crops are ripe. The cowherd has to watch over the cows with close vigilance to prevent them from straying into and feasting on the ripe crops.

Once the crops have been harvested, however, the cowherd can relax and just observe the cows from a distance. All he has to do is to be aware that "there are the cows." For this distant watching the simile uses the term *sati* (Anālayo 2003: 53 and 2014a: 87). I picture the cowherd sitting relaxed at the root of a tree and watching the cows grazing in various places. All he has to do is just be aware of them from an uninvolved distance.

Needless to say, the cowherd will not get awakened by just being aware of the cows. More than just being mindful is required for that. This is precisely where clearly knowing, *sampajañña*, comes in to plant the seeds of wisdom in the fertile soil of mindful observation. In terms of my earlier simile, without the yeast of clearly knowing, the dough of mindfulness practice will result only in flatbread. The wise input provided by clearly knowing marks the difference from the cowherd's mindfulness. Although the cowherd lacks the crucial wisdom part, observing the cows from a distance is nevertheless a good illustration of the receptivity and breadth of mind that I consider to be an important dimension of mindfulness.

The cowherd simile is not alone in conveying this sense. Another relevant discourse is the *Mahātaṇhāsaṅkhaya-sutta*, which relates a narrow state of mind to being without mindfulness of the body. However, a state of mind that is broad, even boundless, comes with mindfulness of the body established (MN 38; Anālayo 2014a: 87 and 2017a: 40). Here the presence of mindfulness of the body clearly relates to a broad state of mind.

The importance of this breadth of mind lies in the comprehensiveness of vision that results from such an open-minded attitude. This is somewhat like taking a picture with a wide-angle lens. Such wide-angle openness allows mental space for differences to exist side by side. The resultant mental spaciousness stands in contrast to the narrow-mindedness of being firmly convinced that our particular view or understanding is the only right one. This does not mean that we are no longer entitled to have an opinion. It does mean, however, that our personal opinions are seen for what they are: just opinions, which may or may not be correct. We learn to allow space for diversity to unfold without suppression or negativity.

With a bit of mindful observation, we can in fact easily notice how spacious and allowing the mind can be when we are open to differences and variety, and how narrow and cramped the mind can become when we are self-righteous and judgemental. Becoming aware of this difference can serve as a good signpost for noticing when the mind shifts from open-mindedness to closing down.

Combining an open-minded attitude with being fully in the present moment requires some form of an anchor. It is a common experience that mindfulness is lost and the mind succumbs to some sort of distraction or fantasy. The challenge here is to find an anchor that supports the continuity of mindfulness without losing the qualities of open-mindedness and receptivity. In other words, the anchor should be established without introducing too strong a focus and without too much of an interfering and controlling attitude.

In my personal experience, I have found the most helpful tool to meet this challenge to be the type of mindfulness mentioned in the *Mahātaṇhāsaṅkhaya-sutta*: mindfulness of the body. In simple terms, mindfulness of the body means a form of mindfulness that in one way or another relates to aspects of the body or to the body as a whole. Needless to say, both modes are interrelated. Becoming aware of parts of the body strengthens whole-body awareness, just as awareness of the whole body easily leads over to awareness of its different parts. Given the need to avoid too strong a focus, however, the mode of mindfulness of the body that recommends itself for serving as an anchor is awareness of the whole physical body.

MINDFULNESS OF BODILY POSTURES

Mindfulness of the whole body can be related to two contemplations in the *Satipaṭṭhāna-sutta*, which describe being aware of the bodily postures and clearly knowing bodily activities (MN 10). The instructions for the first of these two are as follows:

> When walking, one knows: "I am walking"; or when standing, one knows: "I am standing"; or when sitting, one knows: "I am sitting"; or when lying down, one knows: "I am lying down"; or, however the body is disposed, one knows it accordingly.

The passage is not about performing any of these postures in a special way, such as doing slow-motion walking meditation, but just about knowing the postures of the body as they occur naturally. To my mind this conveys the sense of a continuity of awareness of the body combined with clearly knowing its posture. It is something natural and without artificiality; in fact the naturalness helps to avoid going into autopilot mode. This can easily happen when we train ourselves to do something invariably in a particular manner. Natural walking is also what I would recommend for walking meditation by way of just resting in whole-body awareness during the walking process. When walking, we just walk with our whole being.

The ability to know if the body is in one of these four

postures relies on what clinical psychology calls proprioceptive awareness. The term "proprioception" refers to the ability to sense the position of the body and its movements. Even with closed eyes we are able to know the position of our body through this type of ability. It is a felt sense of physical presence. This felt physical presence provides an easily available sense of "here", and mindfulness itself keeps us in the "now". In this way mindfulness of the body can combine spatial and temporal dimensions that facilitate our being fully in the here and now.

During normal daily life this felt sense of physical presence is usually not noticed. It quickly comes to the forefront of attention, however, when bodily balance is lost. Meditative cultivation of this felt sense of physical presence can take place by being aware of the body in any posture. This requires allowing this natural ability of proprioceptive awareness to become a recognized aspect of our experience. In this way neither is it ignored, as usually, nor does it take up the whole field of attention, as is the case when a loss of bodily balance occurs. Such meditative cultivation is not a forceful grabbing hold of the body, but rather a resting in the presence of the whole body. The phrase I tend to use to introduce the flavour of this practice is: "We are aware of the body in the sitting posture and we let the mind rest on the body just as the body rests on the cushion."

Properly cultivated, such mindfulness of the body results in a sense of being firmly grounded in the body; it is an embodied awareness. Such embodied awareness does not need to interfere with other tasks and activities. Instead, it can accompany them. To accomplish this takes training. The natural tendency of the mind is either to focus or to ignore. Proprioceptive awareness can be employed to cultivate a middle path between these two extremes.

Cultivating this middle path comes about by way of a gradual approach, rather than through mere force of the will. Once the centring and balancing potential of mindfulness of the body has become a matter of personal experience, it becomes easier to return to the body even amidst the most challenging situations. The body is always there, wherefore turning mindfulness towards it can serve almost like a portable meditation device, ready at hand in any situation. All it takes is to become aware of some part of the body and from that entry door to allow mindfulness to encompass the whole body, enabling the mind to rest in that encompassing awareness as its reference point. This in itself simple act of turning with awareness to the presence of the body can transform the most boring types of situation into opportunities for practice. Caught up in a traffic jam, sitting in the doctor's waiting room, standing in a long queue at passport control, any such setting can be transformed by embodied mindfulness. Such is the power of this middle path between exclusive focus and distraction.

Advantages of cultivating this middle path are stability and continuity of mindfulness. It enables bridging the gap between formal meditation during a retreat or sitting period and everyday activities. This is decisive. For meditation practice to flourish truly, formal sitting and everyday life have to evolve into an integrated whole, each supporting the other. This can be achieved by finding a way of maintaining the presence of mindfulness, regardless of what needs to be done.

When outer circumstances make continuity of mindfulness difficult, it can be helpful to use a phrase from the part of the *Satipaṭṭhāna-sutta* I call the "refrain". The relevant part reads: "mindfulness is established that 'there is the body'." Just bringing to mind this phrase: "there is the body" (or its Pāli equivalent, *atthi kāyo*) can help to re-establish mindfulness of the body and to support its continuity. The same type of phrase can also be used for the domains of the other *satipaṭṭhānas*. If the situation at hand gives rise to prominent feelings, for example, the mental phrase to be used could be: "there is feeling", *atthi vedanā*.

A good way to get a practical sense of what it means to cultivate such an embodied awareness would be taking a walk in a forest. Walking in the forest, can we just walk in the forest? Is it possible to be fully with the present moment of walking? For the time being, can we leave behind all our concerns and duties, our roles and identities, as well as the ever-active mental commentator within? When walking in the forest, can we just know that we are walking? Based on the resultant rootedness in the act of walking, can we allow the mind to be wide open and receptive to the beauty of nature around us?

Establishing continuity of awareness in the four postures builds the foundation for the next exercise described in the *Satipaṭṭhāna-sutta*, which is clearly knowing in relation to various bodily activities. In this context, clearly knowing refers to a general sense of appropriateness and propriety. The same quality also occurs in the part of the discourse that I like to call the "definition". In that context, clearly knowing seems to have a more specific purpose, which I understand to be in particular to serve as a reminder of the changing nature of all aspects of experience. In terms of my earlier simile, the clearly knowing mentioned in the definition is the yeast required for the bread of insight.

MINDFULNESS OF BODILY ACTIVITIES

The instructions in the *Satipaṭṭhāna-sutta* for the type of clearly knowing that is relevant to various bodily activities proceed as follows:

> When going forward and returning one acts clearly knowing; when looking ahead and looking away one acts clearly knowing; when flexing and extending [the limbs] one acts clearly knowing; when wearing the outer robe and [other] robes and [carrying] the bowl one acts clearly knowing; when eating, drinking, consuming food, and tasting one acts clearly knowing; when defecating and urinating one acts clearly knowing; when walking, standing, sitting, falling asleep, waking up, talking, and keeping silent one acts clearly knowing.

Aspects of this description relate in particular to the lifestyle of a monastic. But by understanding robes to be representative of clothing in general and the bowl to stand in place of any tool to be used, the description can be related to lay practice as well. Clearly knowing (*sampajañña*) has its foundation in the presence of mindfulness. It is only when we are aware of what we are doing that we can do it clearly knowing. The activities described are going somewhere and looking at something, moving our limbs in one way or another, wearing our clothes, eating and drinking, defecating and urinating, going to sleep and waking up, even talking and being silent. Clearly the exercise is meant to embrace all possible kinds of situation. In other words, any situation or activity can in principle become food for mindfulness and clearly knowing.

When turning around to look at something, the Buddha is described as turning around with his whole body, similar to an elephant. This exemplifies wholehearted dedication to an action. Can we eat with our whole body? Can we obey the calls of nature with our whole body? Bringing this fullness of being into any activity has considerable potential. It makes us become more alive. We learn to cultivate the subtle joy of being fully in the present moment through such embodied mindfulness.

Waking up in the morning, we can start right away by being aware of the whole body. Before getting into any other activity, we take a few moments just to be aware of the body lying in the bed. Getting up then involves the other three postures, where from lying down we proceed to sitting, standing, and then walking. In this way we can begin the day with a check-in on whole-body awareness in all four postures, which will enable us to continue the day with a good grounding in embodied mindfulness. Having established such a foundation, it becomes easier to return to mindfulness throughout the day until the time comes to rest again. At that time we proceed through the same four postures in reverse order: walking to reach the bed, standing by its side, sitting down on it, and eventually lying down. All of this can be done with whole-body awareness, until we fall asleep.

Probably the most challenging of the activities mentioned in the passage above is talking. I propose to understand talking here to cover any type of communication, including use of email and internet. The mind can get so active and involved in these activities that we easily forget about mindfulness of the body. Yet, to come back to it only requires a moment of turning inward and becoming aware of the body.

Whole-body awareness can in principle remain present in the background of any activity, including even the most heated discussion. Nevertheless, a heated discussion is probably a rather challenging situation and not the best place to get started with this type of practice. It would be preferable to bring mindfulness gradually into daily activities and situations, in order to avoid frustration arising and undermining our dedication to this crucial dimension of the practice. The outside world offers us a testing ground where we can check on and mature the insights gained in formal meditation. We need to avoid creating a rigid division between formal meditation and ordinary activities. But this testing ground in the world outside is better not seen as a sort of exam which we pass or else become an utter failure. Instead, it is preferable to visualize it more as a playground where we can try out different tactics to see what works for us. From this perspective, it simply works better if we approach everyday situations with a relaxed inner smile, considering whatever occurs as a chance for testing out different ways of being with *sati*.

In order to get started, we might just try to be mindful, from time to time (without immediately aiming at uninterrupted continuity), when hearing or reading the communications of others. Hearing or reading are in themselves more passive activities and therefore more easily amenable to being combined with the receptive and non-interfering attitude of *sati*. Grounded in whole-body awareness, we try to remain balanced and aware of what others are expressing. Every moment we are mindful is a gain, as in this way we have taken another step in the right direction. No need to berate ourselves for those moments when mindfulness was lost. Distraction and getting caught up is a natural tendency of the mind, but every single step taken in the other direction will slowly weaken this tendency.

Experimenting for some time with adorning our lives step by step with the beauty of moments of embodied mindfulness will yield plainly evident benefits in our ability to understand and interact better with others. We also become better at distinguishing between what others express and how this comes to be coloured by our own commentary on it, how our biases tend to interfere even when just hearing or reading. This in turn makes us notice how our own mind wants to react. With the growth of this understanding we in turn feel sufficiently fortified to extend the practice further, by trying to be with mindfulness even when we are actually reacting, be it by writing a message or by saying something. When moving into this more challenging arena of what is yet another dimension of our meditative training, it can be helpful to take a conscious breath that reconnects us with our bodily experience before we begin to write or speak. Hardly noticeable to others, such brief reconnection with a mindful grounding in the body can serve as an inner switch to get our meditative attitude in operation. This meditative attitude can turn any experience, be it at the workplace or at home, into an integral dimension of our progress on the path.

BENEFITS OF MINDFULNESS OF THE BODY

Gradually cultivating this ability eventually provides a strong anchor; it can offer a powerful grounding to face any type of challenge with *sati*. In a way we are never alone as long as *sati* is with us. Her presence will make sure that we stay balanced and centred, helping us to take in fully the relevant information before reacting and enabling us to keep monitoring how we react, noting any loss of balance along the way.

Whenever we forget about *sati* and get caught up in some sort of distraction, what is required is just a moment of smiling recognition. No need for disappointment or a sense of failure, no need for getting upset with ourselves. A smiling realization that the mind has wandered away is quite adequate. This is natural; this is the tendency of the mind. But here is our good friend, *sati*, right here patiently waiting for us to come and be with her again. And being with her is so pleasant, so calm, so spacious; it is just much more attractive than any kind of thought, reaction, or daydream we could entertain in our mind.

With this type of attitude we learn to practise mindfulness of the body with wisdom, knowing very well that it would not be skilful to get tense with the idea: "I must be mindful of the body without any interruption whatsoever." This could in fact be a reflection of the mistaken belief that we are in full control.

From the viewpoint of early Buddhist thought, a key factor in whatever we do is volition or intention. But our volition operates within a wider network of causes and conditions. It can influence things, but it cannot control them completely.

Applied to the experience of distraction, our responsibility is to set up the intention to be mindful and return to that intention whenever we notice that mindfulness has been lost. With that much we have fulfilled our task. If nevertheless the mind is totally distracted, then that is because of other causes and conditions impacting on the present situation. We are simply not in full control within our own mind. On realizing this, we come to appreciate that the best goal to set ourselves is a harmonious balance between our effort to live in the present moment and the natural resistance to that from the tendencies in our mind and from outer circumstances. Instead of the unreasonable expectation that all such resistance should be annihilated once and for all in order for us to qualify as a "good meditator", we inhabit that harmonious balance, where recognition of the manifestation of any resistance is met with the smiling effort that is just sufficient for gently coming back home to the here and now. In this way, instead of turning the cultivation of mindfulness into a stressful and demanding chore, we see *sati* as a good friend to whom we return, with whom we like to spend as much of our time as possible.

Such returning to mindfulness again and again can become a practical expression of the notion in the discourses that the four *satipaṭṭhāna*s provide a refuge within (SN 47.9 or 47.14; Anālayo 2003: 276 and 2013: xiii and 1n3). Embodied mindfulness cultivated in this way does indeed provide an anchor and a refuge throughout the entire day, right up to the moment we fall asleep. It can be there with us right away again the next morning as we wake up. She is always there with her beautiful qualities of receptivity and acceptance, allowing our mind to be broad and spacious. Firmly grounded in the present moment, we can be aware of anything that happens from the vantage point of resting in whole-body awareness.

The nuance of an anchor or a grounding through mindfulness of the body comes to the fore in a simile that describes six different animals that are bound together (SN 35.206; Anālayo 2003: 123 and 2013: 55f). Each of the six animals struggles to go off in a particular direction. The strongest one pulls the others along until it gets tired and another one takes over. This illustrates the fragmentation of our experience by way of the six sense-doors as long as mindfulness of the body is not established. We keep getting pulled here and there, depending on which sense-door has for a moment gathered the greatest strength to take us along.

Establishing mindfulness of the body is like firmly planting a strong post in the ground. However much the six animals struggle to go off in one direction or another, due to being bound to that strong post they will no longer be able to pull the others along. Sooner or later, they will give up pulling and just sit or lie down beside the post.

This illustrates the power of mindfulness of the body. It enables experiencing what is agreeable and what is disagreeable at any of the six sense-doors without getting pulled along. Such ability is particularly crucial for dealing with everyday-life situations. It can be quite tiring to hold the leashes of the six animals. It is more sensible to establish the firm post of mindfulness of the body to take care of the six animals. In this way we can avoid being worn out by them.

During actual practice we just come back to the sense of bodily presence, to proprioceptive awareness, as soon as we realize that we are getting pulled along. In preparation for challenging situations, we make sure first of all that we are aware of the presence of our body. From the vantage point of embodied mindfulness, we become able to face challenges well. This reflects the protective dimension inherent in the establishing of mindfulness (Anālayo 2013: 24ff).

The centredness that results from this form of practice comes to the fore in another simile. This simile describes a person who has to carry a bowl brimful of oil through a crowd. The crowd is watching a dancing and singing performance by a beautiful girl (SN 47.20; Anālayo 2003: 122 and 2013: 56f). Picturing this simile in the ancient Indian context, I imagine that the person is carrying the bowl of oil on the head and that the members of the crowd are trying their best to get really close to the dancing performance to see it well, perhaps even moving to and fro in time with the music.

The simile further specifies that behind the person carrying the oil is someone with a drawn sword. The swordsman is ready to cut off the carrier's head as soon as even a little bit of oil is spilled. To survive this challenging situation, the carrier has to be very careful not to get distracted.

Mindfulness of the body provides the centredness that it takes to survive even the most dangerous and challenging situation. In line with the image of carrying a bowlful of oil on the head, the sense of bodily centredness can be experimented with by, for example, carrying a thick book around on our head. Fortunately nobody will cut off our head, should the book fall to the ground. Doing an experiment of this type can help to get a sense of the bodily centredness that to my mind is a relevant nuance of this simile.

A key aspect of the potential of mindfulness of the body is the providing of a type of anchoring that ensures the continuity of mindfulness without introducing too strong a focus. This is the advantage of whole-body awareness over a form of mindfulness that takes a narrower object, which can easily result in too strong a focus and thereby in losing awareness of the overall situation.

A simile in the *Kāyagatāsati-sutta* explains the relationship between wholesome states leading to knowledge and mindfulness of the body (MN 119; Anālayo 2013: 60). This relationship is similar to that between various rivers and the ocean. The ocean includes all of them. The same inclusiveness comes about through mindfulness of the body.

Imagine standing on a beach and looking out over the ocean. It is so vast and wide. In a similar way, mindfulness of the body can function as a wide-open container for the various rivers of our activities. It can do so by providing a central reference point and support, without interfering with the activity we are engaged in. It also helps to string together whatever we do into a continuous practice, when all our activities take place in the company of our good friend, mindfulness of the body. Her presence is the one taste that can come to pervade all our practice and activities. The ocean has a single taste, which is the taste of salt (AN 8.19; Anālayo 2013: 251). Similarly, continuous establishing of mindfulness of the body can lead to all of our experiences acquiring a single taste, the taste of progress to liberation.

Another simile compares mindfulness to a capable charioteer (SN 45.4; Anālayo 2013: 37). Just like a good driver, we learn to steer the vehicle of our activities through any kind of traffic without running into an accident. The *Kāyagatāsati-sutta* illustrates the ability to avoid such an accident, which would be equivalent to falling into the hands of Māra, with several similes (MN 119; Anālayo 2003: 123 and 2013: 60). These similes depict a fire that is easily made with dry wood, water that is easily poured into an empty pot, and a stone that, on being thrown, easily enters a mound of wet clay. Similarly, Māra will easily get an opportunity to overpower those who have not cultivated mindfulness of the body by setting them on fire as if they were dry wood, filling them up like an empty pot, and throwing something at them that gets in.

When mindfulness of the body has been cultivated, however, Māra no longer gains such an opportunity. Being with mindfulness of the body compares to wet wood that will not burn, to a full pot that will not take any more liquid, and to a solid door panel at which a light ball is thrown without having any effect.

These images bring out how mindfulness of the body can serve as a form of protection. When we are rooted in whole-body awareness, sensually alluring objects do not easily set the mind on fire. Embodied awareness can yield a sense of inner contentment as a source of joy, and being filled with such joy we will not be like an empty pot that takes in anything that comes along just to get filled up. Whatever others may throw at us will just bounce off, instead of entering.

The practice of mindfulness of the body is the hub of the type of practice that I will be presenting in the following pages. This is where we start, where we continue, and where we conclude: maintaining a somatic anchor in the here and now through embodied awareness, which serves as a support for a widely open and receptive mental attitude. Our awareness is fully with the present moment, as if it were of supreme importance to us to be able to remember it. With mindfulness we stay widely open and receptive to whatever manifests at any of the six sense-doors. We are rooted and grounded in the felt physical reality of the whole body. This serves as a container for all our practices, similar to the ocean. Such is the beauty and potential of mindfulness of the body.

SUMMARY

Mindfulness is not a given of any experience, but much rather requires intentional cultivation. During such cultivation, mindfulness can coexist with the use of concepts; in fact the input provided through the wise use of concepts is of crucial importance for *satipaṭṭhāna* meditation. In actual *satipaṭṭhāna* practice, mindfulness is concerned with what is present, not with recollecting matters of the past. The memory connotation of *sati* can be taken to convey the sense that the openly receptive stance of mindfulness should be such that we would later be able to recall easily what happened. In order to provide an anchor for an attitude of open-minded receptivity, mindfulness of the whole body recommends itself.

II

SATIPAṬṬHĀNA

In the introduction I briefly mentioned that, in spite of the amount of detail that I had been able to gather in the course of my research published as *Satipaṭṭhāna, The Direct Path to Realization*, I still felt I was somehow missing the overall picture. The different exercises found under the heading of contemplation of the body and contemplation of dharmas in particular seemed somewhat too complex as a whole for me to get a clear sense of the thrust of these two *satipaṭṭhāna*s.

FOUR *SATIPAṬṬHĀNA*S

Yet another stumbling block for me was that all four *satipaṭṭhāna*s are combined into a single unified practice in the *Ānāpānasati-sutta* (MN 118; Anālayo 2003: 133ff, 2013: 227ff, and forthcoming b). Based on the breath, which in itself is a bodily phenomenon, a continuous and seamless progression of meditation leads from one *satipaṭṭhāna* to the next.

I was unable to see how a similar progression could be achieved in actual practice based on the *Satipaṭṭhāna-sutta*. Surveying the contemplations listed in the discourse, it was not evident to me how they could be developed as a seamless form of practice that mirrors the continuity evident in the *Ānāpānasati-sutta*. In a way it seemed to me only natural that at present *satipaṭṭhāna* tends to be taught based on selecting one or perhaps two *satipaṭṭhānas*, but not by covering all four.

Yet, the four right efforts, for example, corresponding to factor six of the noble eightfold path, clearly build on and complement each other. The same holds for the four absorptions, listed regularly in descriptions of right concentration as factor eight of the same path. I was unable to envisage how the four *satipaṭṭhānas* as factor seven of this path could similarly be practised as building on and complementing each other.

Could there be a way of bringing all four *satipaṭṭhānas* together into a unified continuous mode of practice? Would it not be possible to develop a seamless continuity with each *satipaṭṭhāna* building on the next, complementing one another? Is there at the same time a simple mode of practice that can be carried into any situation? Such questions were very much on my mind.

The solution came to me through a detailed study of the Chinese parallels. This is the topic of my second book, *Perspectives on Satipaṭṭhāna*. In principle the discourses found in the Chinese *Āgamas* have just as much of a claim as the Pāli discourses to being an authentic record of the teachings of the Buddha and his disciples (leaving aside translation errors). Placing the *Satipaṭṭhāna-sutta* side by side with its two Chinese parallels enabled me to discover the common ground between them and the differences.

Although the next chapters will be based on the Pāli version, the comparative perspective that I gained from studying the Chinese parallels informs my approach. Since the present book is predominantly meant as a guide for meditation practice, I will not mention all of the variations in the parallels. The relevant information in this respect can be found in my other publications, to which I will be referring in the course of my discussion.

Perhaps at this point it might also be good to mention that the undertaking of such comparison with parallel versions does not mean that what is not found in all versions should just be rejected. It is more like positioning different pieces before our eyes, placing them either towards the front or more towards the back. In other words, those exercises that are common to the parallel versions can be in the foreground and allowed to become more prominent as expressions of a particular *satipaṭṭhāna*. Other exercises not found in all versions simply stand somewhat more in the background.

CONTEMPLATION OF THE BODY

Based on such positioning, three exercises emerge as the common ground of body contemplation. These are contemplation of the anatomical parts, of the elements, and of a corpse in decay. I understand these three to stand for the cultivation of insight into three dimensions of the nature of the body. The first deconstructs projections of beauty and sexual attractiveness onto the body (be it our own or that of others). The second reveals the empty nature of material existence as manifest in the body (as well as outside of it). The third drives home the mortality of the body (be it our own or that of others).

An alternative approach to the third contemplation could be to take the stages of decay of a corpse to highlight the body's inherent lack of beauty. Since this topic has already been covered by contemplation of the anatomy, and in view of the importance of facing our own death, however, my own approach to this exercise is to cultivate it as a pointer to mortality.

With the three contemplations of the anatomical parts, of the elements, and of a corpse in decay, the first *satipaṭṭhāna* clearly becomes a way of cultivating insight into the nature of the body. In other words, the task here is not so much using the body to cultivate mindfulness, but rather using *satipaṭṭhāna* contemplation to cultivate a lessening of attachment to the body.

The basic thrust of contemplation of the body also emerges from a discourse in the *Satipaṭṭhāna-saṃyutta*, which recommends that *satipaṭṭhāna* should be taught to beginners who have just ordained (SN 47.4; Anālayo 2003: 271 and 2013: 159). In the case of the first *satipaṭṭhāna*, beginners should practise in such a way that they understand the body as it really is (*yathābhūta*). Those more advanced in the training continue the same practice for the sake of a penetrative understanding (*pariññā*) of the body. Fully awakened ones still cultivate contemplation of the body; they do so being free from any attachment to it. Needless to say, the continuous relevance of contemplation from the beginner's cultivation all the way up to an arahant's freedom of attachment applies similarly to the other three *satipaṭṭhānas*. In the case of the body, then, from a practical perspective the task is indeed to understand it as it really is. Such understanding becomes increasingly more penetrative in such a way that it results in gradually eroding all attachments to the body.

This is not to say that using the body to cultivate mindfulness has no importance. On the contrary, this is an essential dimension of practice. In fact exercises like mindfulness of the four postures and clearly knowing bodily activities have a remarkable potential. Much of what I said in the previous chapter is precisely about this potential. But, in order to cultivate *satipaṭṭhāna* in such a way that it becomes the direct path to liberation, the type of insight that can be developed with these three contemplations of the body offers a major contribution.

CONTEMPLATION OF DHARMAS

The situation with contemplation of dharmas also shows substantial differences (with contemplation of feelings and the mind the parallels are fairly close to each other). Strictly speaking, what remains as the common core of this contemplation in the *Satipaṭṭhāna-sutta* and its two Chinese discourse parallels is the cultivation of the awakening factors. I add to this also contemplation of the hindrances, as this is found in two versions and at least referred to in the third. In fact, cultivation of the awakening factors requires having first of all recognized and then overcome the hindrances, at any rate their gross manifestations.

The impression that emerges from foregrounding the awakening factors, together with the hindrances, is that contemplation of dharmas is about monitoring the mental qualities that obstruct and those that lead forward on the path to liberation. In other words, contemplation of dharmas is about the type of mind in which awakening can (or cannot) take place.

This perspective helped me to build a bridge to contemplation of dharmas in the *Ānāpānasati-sutta*, where the task is to cultivate insight perspectives alongside awareness of the changing nature of the breath. These insight perspectives are to contemplate impermanence, dispassion, cessation, and letting go. Cultivation of the awakening factors in such a way that they will fulfil their awakening potential similarly requires proceeding through the themes of dispassion and cessation, culminating in letting go. In this way, reading side by side the sections on contemplation of dharmas in the *Satipaṭṭhāna-sutta* and the *Ānāpānasati-sutta* points to those mental qualities and insight topics that are particularly helpful for the realization of Nibbāna.

SEVEN CONTEMPLATIONS

This understanding of the basic thrust of each *satipaṭṭhāna* has helped me to resolve the questions I had. The remainder of this book is dedicated to depicting how in actual meditation a seamless continuity in the practice of all four *satipaṭṭhāna*s can be achieved. This takes place by progressing through these seven topics:

- anatomy,
- elements,
- death,
- feelings,
- mind,
- hindrances,
- awakening (factors).

The first three cover contemplation of the body, the fourth and fifth correspond to contemplation of feelings and of the mind respectively, and the last two are modes of contemplation of dharmas.

The perspective afforded in this way by comparative study has a precedent in the Theravāda Abhidharma. The *Vibhaṅga* in fact presents an even shorter version of *satipaṭṭhāna*. This includes only the anatomical parts for contemplation of the body and just the hindrances and the awakening factors for contemplation of dharmas (Vibh 193; Anālayo 2003: 121 and 240 and 2013: 53 and 175).

I would like to stress again that leaving out some of the exercises mentioned in the *Satipaṭṭhāna-sutta* and instead focusing on those that are common to all versions does not imply any form of devaluation. The purpose is simply to allow a focus on what seems most essential. In fact the mode of practice I will be presenting in this book also covers central aspects and themes of the exercises that are not explicitly included.

One practice not included concerns the four steps of mindfulness of breathing that in the whole scheme of sixteen steps in the *Ānāpānasati-sutta* correspond to contemplation of the body. In relation to contemplation of the corpse, the instructions I present incorporate awareness of the process of breathing as a reminder of mortality. In this way, directing mindfulness to the breath is still part of contemplation of the body in the form I am presenting it here, even though it does not feature as an exercise on its own and does not involve the sixteen steps.

The same implicit inclusion holds for contemplation of bodily postures and clearly knowing bodily activities. As mentioned in the previous chapter, the gist of these two exercises naturally emerges due to the central importance given to mindfulness of the whole body in the mode of practice I describe here.

Similar to the three contemplations of the body that are not explicitly included, three contemplations of dharmas from the *Satipaṭṭhāna-sutta* are also not in the above list of seven topics. One of these concerns directing mindfulness to the impermanent nature of the five aggregates. Such awareness nevertheless builds up naturally with my instructions for the first three *satipaṭṭhānas*. With contemplation of the mind, these instructions culminate in a comprehensive meditative experience of the impermanent nature of all aspects of experience, encompassing body, feeling, perceptions, thoughts, and mental states. The net result of such practice is fairly similar to contemplation of the arising and passing away of the five aggregates described in the *Satipaṭṭhāna-sutta*.

The main mode of practice I recommend adopting after having worked through the specific exercises is open awareness of whatever happens at any sense-door, based on remaining grounded in whole-body mindfulness. This fulfils central elements of contemplation of the six sense-spheres as described in the *Satipaṭṭhāna-sutta*, which is concerned in particular with drawing attention to the fettering force of sense experience.

The four noble truths, although not taken up explicitly, underlie the approach to the four *satipaṭṭhāna*s I present. I will come back to this topic in the conclusion (see below p. 206ff), as appreciating this correlation requires familiarity with the details of the implementation of the four *satipaṭṭhāna*s I present in the chapters between the present and the last.

MINDFULNESS IN DAILY LIFE

The progression through the seven practices that I take up explicitly converges on an element of simplicity: mindfulness of the whole body. I visualize the practice I present in the ensuing pages as a wheel, which I will be referring to as "the wheel of practice". This wheel has seven spokes, which are the seven *satipaṭṭhāna* contemplations: the three bodily spokes of contemplating the anatomical parts, the elements, and a corpse in decay, followed by one spoke each for the contemplations of feelings, mental states, the hindrances, and the awakening factors. The hub of this wheel is mindfulness of the body.

Mindfulness of the body as the hub of the wheel is the entry door into a simple mode of practice that can be undertaken in any situation. Whatever we may be doing, the *body* is there. Becoming aware of the body in the way I recommend here is to sense the body, to *feel* it. Being aware of that felt sense of bodily presence takes place in a *mental state* of awareness of the present moment. Every moment of cultivating this practice and relating it in some way to insight is yet another step forward on the path to liberation, reflecting the main thrust of the fourth *satipaṭṭhāna*.

In short, in any situation we can simply touch down on some aspect of the body, thereby coming back to the presence of the body. Feeling it and being aware of the mind that knows the felt presence of the body can be considered as establishing the three-dimensionality of the first three *satipaṭṭhāna*s in daily life. The fourth dimension, which is to relate the whole situation to progress to liberation, comes through the awareness that whatever happens is a changing process, it is impermanent.

Time is in a way our conceptualization of change. Past, present, and future are what has changed, what is changing, and what will change. Measuring time in units, however useful it may be, can at times come with an underlying nuance of attempting to control change. Yet, in the end, we invariably find that change is outside of our control. In this way, we end up being controlled by our own conceptualizations of time. Time becomes what we never seem to get enough of. Always under time pressure, always under stress, we keep having "no time". Simply becoming aware of change, of the process character of all our experience, helps to counter this tendency. It undermines our unconscious attempt to control change and it frees us from taking time too seriously. This makes us less vulnerable to time-related stress.

Combining central aspects of all four *satipaṭṭhānas* into a single and simple mode of practice facilitates maintaining continuity between detailed *satipaṭṭhāna* contemplations, usually undertaken during formal meditation, and everyday situations. Basic awareness of these four domains of *satipaṭṭhāna* meditation in daily life can, according to the situation and our personal needs, lead on to a closer look at any of these four. *Feeling* the body can lead on to exploring other feelings, if this seems appropriate. A *mental state* of present-moment awareness offers an easy entry door into recognizing the condition of our own mind, should this be relevant. The orientation towards awakening as the central driving force of contemplation of dharmas, encapsulated in being aware of change, can lead to relating what takes place to the teachings in one way or another.

The cultivation of whole-body awareness can combine with occasional focus. An example could be listening to a whole orchestra performing music. Within that performance, a solo has its place. Still, the music of the soloist stands out against the background of the silence of the other instruments. The very same performance by this musician would be different if the other members of the orchestra were not present. That sense

of suspense, waiting for the other members of the orchestra to join, would no longer be there.

Similarly, within the framework of the vast and open receptivity of mindfulness that is grounded in the body, focusing on a single aspect has its place. The only requirement is that this focus should remain grounded within a comprehensive awareness of the whole situation, instead of standing in contrast to it. There is no need for the other members of the orchestra to leave the stage when the soloist performs. In fact it is their very silent presence that enhances the performance of the soloist. In the same way, there is no need for whole-body awareness to be abandoned as soon as we decide to focus on one particular aspect of experience. With practice, it will become increasingly easy for us to focus without losing the overall picture.

THE DEFINITION AND THE REFRAIN

According to a part of the instructions in the *Satipaṭṭhāna-sutta* that I like to refer to as the "definition", practising each of the four *satipaṭṭhānas* requires bringing into being the following four qualities:

- diligence,
- clearly knowing,
- mindfulness,
- freedom from desires and discontent (literally: covetousness and sadness) with regard to the world.

The quality of *mindfulness* in the mode of practice I present here is in particular mindfulness grounded in proprioceptive awareness of the body. A primary aspect of *diligence* is in my understanding the effort to meet the present moment in its internal and external dimensions with sustained interest. The quality of *clearly knowing* comes to the forefront through acknowledging the changing nature of the present moment. This nourishes the seeds of insight into impermanence, which build the foundation for insight into *dukkha* and not-self. Such insight is precisely what enables us to become increasingly *free from desires and discontent with regard to the world*.

The relevance of impermanence for each and every *satipaṭṭhāna* emerges from another part of the instructions, which I like to call the "refrain". In the case of body contemplation, this proceeds as follows (MN 10):

> In regard to the body one abides contemplating the body internally, or in regard to the body one abides contemplating the body externally, or in regard to the body one abides contemplating the body internally and externally.

> Or one abides contemplating the nature of arising in the body, or one abides contemplating the nature of passing away in the body, or one abides contemplating the nature of arising and passing away in the body.

> Or mindfulness that "there is a body" is established in one just for the sake of bare knowledge and continuous mindfulness.

And one abides independently, not clinging to anything in the world.

The following four domains of *satipaṭṭhāna* practice emerge:

- contemplate internally, externally, and both,
- contemplate the nature of arising, passing away, and both,
- establish mindfulness just to know and be mindful,
- dwell independently, without clinging to anything.

INTERNAL AND EXTERNAL

The implications of the reference to internal and external practice are not immediately obvious. Various interpretations have been proposed (Anālayo 2003: 94–102). What remains certain is that this part of the refrain points to the need to be comprehensive in our cultivation of *satipaṭṭhāna*.

The interpretation that, to my mind, makes the most sense from a practical viewpoint is to take "external" as referring to others. Our own body is made up of anatomical parts and elements, and after death will go through the stages of decay of a corpse. The same holds for the bodies of others. We react to certain experiences with pleasant, unpleasant, or neutral feelings (the last is more literally "not-painful-not-pleasant", *adukkhamasukha*), and so do others. We experience certain mental states, including the hindrances and awakening factors, and so do others.

Although to be able to sense directly the feelings and mental states of others would require telepathic powers, at least a basic degree of recognition can be achieved through external observation (DN 18; Anālayo 2003: 96f and 2013: 17f). It is possible for us to understand from the facial expression, bodily posture, and tone of voice if another person is experiencing pleasant, unpleasant, or neutral feelings. It is similarly possible, through reliance on such external observation, to have an idea of what is most likely going on in the mind of another.

Here sustained cultivation of awareness of the whole body has an additional benefit to offer. A natural result of the increased attention given to our own bodily posture and activities is that those of others also receive more than average attention. This in turn makes us more easily become aware of what others communicate on the bodily level. At times this can be a better guide to assessing what is happening for them on the feeling and mental level than what they say. In this way, the practice of mindfulness of the body can become a helpful tool for better understanding and interacting with others.

Adopting the proposed interpretation of the qualification "external" as referring to others would imply understanding any contemplated phenomenon from the viewpoint of its internal and external manifestations. By shifting from internal to external we increasingly learn to broaden our perspective from seeing only our own subjective viewpoint to taking into account the viewpoints of others. When interpersonal conflicts arise, we learn to be aware not only of our needs, of what we would like to happen and where we feel we have been wronged, but also of how the situation appears to others. What are their needs? In what ways do they feel they have been wronged? What would they like to happen? More and more we learn to understand the many ways in which others are impacted by what we do and say. In this way, formal meditation and mindfulness in daily life seamlessly merge, building on the embodied presence of mindfulness. Mindfulness of the body forms a backdrop for anything that happens, building a bridge between sitting practice and various activities.

External contemplation of this type would be more relevant for everyday life and less a matter of formal sitting meditation. Even a Buddhist monastic living in seclusion will have to go out daily to collect alms food and join the monastic community every fortnight for the recital of the code of rules (Anālayo 2017a: 37f). Thus occasions for such external contemplation manifest naturally, even more so for the average lay practitioner in the modern world.

The external dimension in the cultivation of mindfulness makes an important contribution to the growth of insight. In the end, what counts is the degree to which any insight leads to actual transformation. For this to happen, insights gained during formal meditation need to be applied in daily life. They should be put to the test when facing the vicissitudes and challenges that occur outside of the seclusion of formal meditation and retreat. Such putting to the test will enable discerning the true value of any insight and ensure that it becomes so ingrained within, through repeated application, that it indeed effects substantial and lasting transformation.

Another aspect of the distinction between internal and external *satipaṭṭhāna* meditation is to reinforce a relationship drawn in the previous chapter between mindfulness and breadth of mind. It is precisely the wide-angle vision cultivated in this way that naturally leads to contemplating any particular phenomenon from both perspectives combined: internally and externally. Taking the case of anger as an example: how does it feel when I get angry? How will others feel when they get angry? How do I feel when others get angry at me? How will others feel when I get angry at them?

Only when we take into account these complementary perspectives do we really understand how painful anger is. Since the external dimension of the manifestation of anger will most likely show up outside of formal sitting meditation, another point from the last chapter comes up again here. This is the pressing need to develop a form of practice that enables bringing the qualities of mindful observation into daily life. For *satipaṭṭhāna* meditation, daily activities and interactions are crucial training grounds.

Nevertheless, the instructions mention first the "internal" and then the "external". This gives the impression that familiarity with the contemplated phenomenon is first of all to be established in relation to ourselves, before contemplating the same in its external dimension. In other words, the pressing need to bring mindfulness into daily life should not become an excuse for neglecting formal sitting. First of all we establish some degree of expertise within, then we are ready to move out into the world. Having moved out into the world, we return again to the meditation seat to deepen our practice further, and so on.

A simile that can be taken to illustrate the progression from the internal to the external dimensions of mindfulness practice describes the cooperation of two acrobats (SN 47.19; Anālayo 2003: 276, 2013: 244ff, and 2017a: 13ff). The two acrobats need to take care to establish first of all their own balance. Based on such internal balance, they are able to take care of the other and perform well. Similarly, internal practice of *satipaṭṭhāna* builds the indispensable foundation for being able to remain established in *satipaṭṭhāna* when dealing with others. In this way, facing the outside world will naturally lead to increasing degrees of patience and kindness, precisely through the foundation laid in mindfulness practice.

Although proceeding from the internal to the external offers a meaningful progression, this does not imply that it is in principle impossible to proceed from the external to the internal. A case known to me personally illustrates this. A woman had a severely handicapped baby, which among other problems was blind and deaf. Taking care of her child for many years, she learned to pay very close attention to whatever the child seemed to experience on the bodily, feeling, and mental level. When she subsequently came to sit a course on *satipaṭṭhāna*, she immediately felt she was in familiar terrain. Her child had in a way already taught her about the first three *satipaṭṭhāna*s. Having already developed familiarity with the external dimension of mindfulness practice, it was easy for her to explore the internal dimension as well as to broaden the perspective by bringing in the fourth *satipaṭṭhāna*.

The formulation of this first part of the refrain comes with a doubling of the reference to the body: in regard to the body, we abide contemplating the body. The same holds for the other three *satipaṭṭhāna*s. A similar doubling is also found in relation to the individual contemplations to which I will turn in subsequent chapters. I understand this doubling to imply that, out of the whole range of bodily phenomena, particular instances are selected for closer observation. In this way the refrain, as well as the individual exercises, share a concern with specific aspects. To return to my earlier example, anger is one particular mental state. To understand this state requires clear recognition of the presence or absence of anger and of its manifestations internally and externally.

The relationship between the individual *satipaṭṭhāna* contemplations and mindfulness of the body in daily life can be illustrated with the example of a lotus flower. When the sun shines the petals open and the whole beauty of the flower and its fragrance manifests. This represents the experience and depth of practice in formal meditation when working with the individual contemplations to explore the internal dimension of *satipaṭṭhāna*. At other times the petals close and we still see the outer parts of the petal but no longer smell the fragrance. This stands for mindfulness in everyday life, which affords us an opportunity to explore the external dimension of *satipaṭṭhāna*. Whether opened or closed, it remains the same flower. Similarly, the internal and external complement each other. At the same time, there is a difference between directly experiencing something within and observing it externally. Likewise, when the petals close, the whole beauty of the lotus is now more within. Only when the petals open do we fully experience the fragrance of the lotus, which represents the distinct flavour of direct experience within.

As practice progresses, the distinction between internal and external dissolves and we contemplate "internally and externally". This serves to clarify that the distinction between "internal" and "external" modes of practice is not meant to encourage the construction of a sharp dichotomy, the creation of two watertight compartments unrelated to each other. Instead, the internal borders on the external and vice versa; the two terms simply refer to parts of what is after all a continuum of experience. In practical terms, to stay with my earlier example, with practice undertaken "internally and externally" we are just aware of "anger" manifesting, regardless of whether this manifestation is within or without.

Inasmuch as the external mode of *satipaṭṭhāna* tends to be more prominent in daily-life practice and the internal in formal meditation, the coming together of the two with contemplation undertaken "internally and externally" exemplifies the fact that in principle there need not be a conflict between these two settings. Instead, once mindfulness is well established, formal meditation imbues daily activities and transforms them. Daily activities in turn offer a touchstone and training ground for whatever insight has emerged in formal sitting, enabling it to deepen on a very practical and personal level. These two dimensions are part of a continuum of practice. To view them as such helps to discern the single thread of embodied mindfulness that can unite them into a harmonious whole.

With sustained practice, what comes to us from the domain of the external need no longer be experienced as a disturbance, but can be harmoniously integrated as food for our awareness. Even outside of formal meditation, mindfulness can remain so well established that we notice clearly what happens internally, how we react on the mental level. With *satipaṭṭhāna* cultivated internally and externally, everything becomes part of a continuous practice and we are more and more at ease among the vicissitudes of life, as if we were fish in water.

THE NATURE OF ARISING AND PASSING AWAY

The second domain of the refrain has no doubling of the reference to the body (or feelings, mind, and dharmas). I understand this to imply that practice now moves from particular aspects to what they all have in common. They are all of a nature to arise and pass away. Here the task is to recognize the process character of all aspects of experience. Noticing when anger has arisen, to stay with the same example, leads on to noticing when it has passed away. Through having recognized the presence and absence of an individual mental state like anger, we come to appreciate that the nature of arising of mental states has its complement in the nature of their passing away (the same holds for the body, feelings, or dharmas). All of these share the nature to arise and pass away.

This part of the refrain is of considerable significance, as it points to a direct experience of the impermanent nature of all aspects of experience. It is perhaps for this reason that a discourse in the *Satipaṭṭhāna-saṃyutta* draws a distinction between *satipaṭṭhāna* and the cultivation (*bhāvanā*) of *satipaṭṭhāna* (SN 47.40; Anālayo 2003: 104). The four contemplations of body, feelings, mind, and dharmas are *satipaṭṭhāna*, ways of "establishing mindfulness". The "cultivation" of these four modes of establishing mindfulness takes place through contemplating the nature of arising, of passing away, and of both in relation to each of these four. In other words, the foundation laid by way of *establishing* mindfulness of the body, feelings, mind, and dharmas should lead on to *cultivating* insight into impermanence in order to actualize the liberating potential of mindfulness practice.

Here it is of further practical significance that the instructions speak of contemplating *the nature* of arising, *the nature* of passing away, and *the nature* of arising and passing away. I take this to imply that the instructions can be fulfilled even if we should miss the actual moment of arising or the actual moment of passing away. Due to the swiftness of such moments, being aware when this actually happens is not easy. Instead, from a practical viewpoint these instructions can be understood to cover also the retrospective realization that a particular phenomenon has arisen and is now present or else that in the meantime it has passed away and is now no longer present. This much would suffice to realize that this phenomenon is indeed of *the nature* to arise and pass away, even if it should not have been possible to catch it exactly at the time it arose or at the time it passed away.

Just as with the internal and external dimensions of practice, here, too, the terms "arising" and "passing away" do not reflect a fundamental dichotomy but rather refer to dimensions in a continuum of changing experience. Practice proceeds from the more easily noticed arising of things to noting their passing away, thereby ensuring that we do not settle into a cosy self-complacency about the nicety of things that arise, but also fully take home the considerably less cosy aspect of impermanence, namely that things pass away, that sooner or later they come to an end.

These two dimensions converge in the awareness of continuous change as the "arising and passing away" of all aspects of experience. The average perspective of the untrained mind is to focus on what arises, what is new and fresh, whereas what is old, passes away, and ceases is avoided. Shifting from "arising" to "passing away" helps to counter this unbalanced perspective. Once balance has been established, the final aim is to see both aspects as parts of a continuum. In short, without any exception body, feelings, mental states, and dharmas are changing phenomena, they arise and pass away. In this way, genuine insight into the all-pervasive process character of experience becomes firmly established.

Such awareness of change comes with a built-in pointer towards emptiness. Seeing the arising and passing away of phenomena we increasingly learn to let go, in the sense of no longer holding on to one thing or another as something that "is" (or "is not"). It is impossible to point to anything as a self-sufficient and independent entity that exists on its own. All is simply an arising and a passing away. How meaningless it is to try to hold on to changing phenomena. How meaningless it is to fight and quarrel. How meaningless it is to try to enforce control and get everything exactly as we want. After all, even if we are successful, it will all change again soon enough.

In a way the first and second domain of the "refrain" can be considered to lay out the ground of the world of our *satipaṭṭhāna* experience. The internal and external contemplations cover the spatial dimension of contemplated phenomena, arising and passing away the temporal dimension of their constant change.

JUST BEING MINDFUL

The third domain of practice mentioned in the refrain concerns being mindful just for the sake of knowing and mindfulness. In actual practice, I suggest implementing this by shifting from working with the individual exercises to a less structured form of meditation. We just rest in open awareness of whatever happens, without choosing or rejecting. As mentioned in the previous chapter, we are just receptively aware that "there is the body", "there is feeling", "there is the mind", and "there are dharmas". This is in a way similar to the cowherd who is just aware that the cows are there. Such practice differs from the cowherd's awareness inasmuch as it builds on the previously established comprehensive vision of the internal and external as well as on the crucial insight into impermanence. This is mentioned just before the present passage in the refrain. It also builds on other dimensions of insight developed with the individual exercises.

In this way, there seems to be a place for "bare awareness" in the *Satipaṭṭhāna-sutta* (Anālayo 2017a: 25f and 2018a). But this place comes after comprehensive meditative vision and experiential insight into impermanence have been cultivated and established. To recapitulate, *satipaṭṭhāna* contemplation begins by cultivating a clear understanding in the internal domain of the body, feelings, etc., and then complements this by also covering the external domain. Both together lead up to a level of understanding that steps out of the dualistic contrast between myself and others, involving a shift towards seeing just the general nature we all share, independently of whether this manifests internally or externally. Such seeing of things from the viewpoint of their general nature leads on to noticing in particular their nature to arise, and then also their nature to pass away. In line with the shift from either internal or external to internal-and-external, here, too, a shift takes place towards arising-and-passing-away, towards continuously seeing impermanence.

It is with insight well established in regard to the spatial and temporal dimensions of the meditative experience in this way that the practice of just being mindful stands in its proper place. It can unfold its transformative potential because it is based on a groundwork in understanding and insight. This groundwork ensures that such bare awareness does not fall into the trap of the cowherd's mindfulness, of just watching without any deeper understanding.

For appreciating this third domain of practice, I find it helpful to keep in mind that the seven individual contemplations do not mention mindfulness in their descriptions of the meditative activities to be undertaken. The instructions are that one "knows" (*pajānāti*). With the anatomical parts and elements one "examines" (*paccavekkhati*), and with the corpse contemplations one "compares" (*upasaṃharati*). Mindfulness is mentioned as the first of the awakening factors, but in this case, too, the actual task is that one "knows".

I understand this to imply that in the present context *sati* is not so much something we *do*, but rather something we *are*. As briefly mentioned in the previous chapter, the different contemplations in the *Satipaṭṭhāna-sutta* serve to establish mindfulness. What we *do* is to know, to examine, and to compare. All of these activities contribute to, converge on, and have their grounding in *being* mindful. Mindfulness itself here does not stand for an activity, but rather for a quality. This one quality remains behind each of the exercises and at the same time forms their consummation.

Aside from its occurrence in the definition as one of the crucial qualities for *satipaṭṭhāna* meditation, it is in the present part of the refrain that mindfulness is explicitly mentioned. With this third part of the refrain we practise for the sake of being continuously mindful. Compared to the preceding two domains of the refrain, the present one points to simply remaining aware of the natural unfolding of the meditative experience.

In the original Pāli, the first three domains of the refrain are connected with one another through the disjunctive particle *vā*, "or". I take this to imply that these are three alternative modes of practice. At the same time, the sequence of presentation seems to suggest that these three alternatives build on one another in a natural progression. This natural progression proceeds from establishing comprehensiveness, via acknowledging change, to just being mindful.

DWELLING INDEPENDENTLY

The final part of the refrain no longer comes with the disjunctive particle "or", but rather with the conjunctive particle *ca*, "and". This is the one out of the four domains that is relevant to any type of *satipaṭṭhāna* meditation: not clinging to anything in the world. It is the gist of the whole practice. Here the "world" is the world of experience. The crucial question regarding this world is not "to be or not to be", but "to cling or not to cling".

Experiencing even a moment of the independence described here is a foretaste of liberation. This is the goal we are practising for. This is the measuring rod for progress. What really counts is not special experiences, however profound they may seem. What really counts is the degree to which we can dwell without clinging to anything.

With mindfulness of the body as the hub and the seven contemplations as the spokes of the wheel of practice, dwelling independently without clinging is the outer rim. Wherever the rim touches the ground, which represents what is happening in the present moment, it is precisely at this point that we need to remain without clinging. Such absence of clinging has the hub of the wheel as its source of strength and the seven spokes as its support. As the wheel keeps moving forward on the path to liberation, wherever the rim touches outer reality the task remains: never cling to anything!

The four domains of the refrain and the four qualities mentioned in the definition could be combined. Contemplating *internal and external* requires *diligent* effort. Recognizing *arising and passing away* calls for *clearly knowing*. Being *mindful* finds its most eloquent expression when we are *mindful just for the sake of knowing and being mindful*. Remaining free *from desires and discontent with regard to the world* matches *dwelling independently, without clinging to anything*.

The key aspects of *satipaṭṭhāna* meditation that emerge from combining the definition and the refrain could be summarized as follows:

- diligently contemplate internally and externally;
- clearly know arising and passing away;
- be mindful just for the sake of knowing and mindfulness;
- remain free from desires and discontent so as to dwell independently, without clinging to anything.

A further condensation for actual practice could simply be: "keep calmly knowing change." Here "keep" reflects diligence in exploring the internal and external dimensions of practice. The need to remain free from desires and discontent and the ability to dwell independently without clinging are summarized in the qualification "calmly". Mindfulness just for the sake of continuous dwelling with mindfulness furnishes the foundation for clearly "knowing", which as a general quality relevant to all *satipaṭṭhāna* practices has as its main task the recognition that whatever is experienced is a manifestation of "change". In this way, "keep calmly knowing change" can serve as a simple guiding principle for *satipaṭṭhāna* practice, and the aim of such practice would be: "never cling to anything".

SUMMARY

Based on the comparative study of the early discourses, seven contemplations emerge as the core of *satipaṭṭhāna* meditation. These can be combined into a continuous mode of practice, comparable to the meditative progression in the *Ānāpānasati-sutta*. The four *satipaṭṭhānas* can also be brought into daily-life situations. Becoming aware of the *body* through *feeling* it, based on a *mental state* in which mindfulness is well established, can serve to activate the first three *satipaṭṭhānas*. The fourth falls into place when whatever is experienced becomes an occasion for the cultivation of liberating insight, which can take the form of noting the impermanent nature of whatever is happening.

Key aspects of *satipaṭṭhāna* practice, described in the "definition" and the "refrain" of the *Satipaṭṭhāna-sutta*, could be summarized as pointing to the need to combine a diligent exploration of internal and external dimensions of the situation at hand with clearly knowing its impermanent nature. In this way mindfulness can be practised for its own sake in such a way that we remain free from desires and discontent and thereby dwell independently without clinging to anything.

III

ANATOMY

The first of the seven spokes in the wheel of *satipaṭṭhāna* practice described in this book takes up the anatomical constitution of the body. The instructions in the *Satipaṭṭhāna-sutta* are as follows (MN 10):

> One examines this same body up from the soles of the feet and down from the top of the hair, enclosed by skin and full of many kinds of impurity: "In this body there are head hairs, body hairs, nails, teeth, skin, flesh, sinews, bones, bone-marrow, kidneys, heart, liver, diaphragm, spleen, lungs, bowels, mesentery, contents of the stomach, faeces, bile, phlegm, pus, blood, sweat, fat, tears, grease, spittle, snot, oil of the joints, and urine."

The present and the other two body contemplations taken up in the next two chapters are meant as aids to cultivate ways of relating to the body without clinging. Elsewhere I have discussed in more detail how early Buddhist meditation theory shows a range of perspectives on the body (Anālayo 2017a: 43ff). The deconstruction of the perception of the body as sensually alluring, which underpins the present exercise, is not the only perspective. It finds its complements in the practice of mindfulness of the body as a neutral way of relating to the body and in the experience of the body pervaded by bliss and happiness during absorption.

THE NATURE OF THE BODY

It is against the background of these complementary perspectives that the evaluative element in the present exercise is best appreciated. In the extract translated above this evaluation takes the form of directing attention to the body as being "impure" (*asuci*), which could alternatively also be translated as "dirty".

In order to appreciate this type of qualification, it can be helpful to turn to a standard recollection to be practised by monastics in relation to their requisites (Anālayo 2017a: 47). This recollection draws attention to the fact that requisites become dirty through contact with our own body. On reflection this turns out to be actually true. Clothes and bedding do become dirty through use, and a major source of that dirt is our own body. Although this is an aspect of the physical body that in contemporary society we are not accustomed to paying attention to, it can hardly be denied. Actually the main thrust of this exercise is precisely to question the way we have become accustomed to relating to human bodies.

An alternative qualification of the same type of exercise speaks of the body as being "not beautiful" (*asubha*). The significance of this qualification in the present context is the notion of beauty as something that is sexually attractive and alluring. It is the type of beauty that arouses the wish to touch, kiss, and have sex. The target of the exercise is not to put into question aesthetic beauty in general. In fact in a discourse in the *Saṃyutta-nikāya* the Buddha eulogizes the physical beauty of a monk he happens to see at that moment (SN 21.5; Anālayo 2017a: 52). This passage clearly shows that there is no problem with beauty as such. The problem rather lies in sensual desire.

Only a minority of human beings fit the tight mould of modern expectations of physical beauty. It is simply unfair that the majority of human beings are discriminated against because they are too plump or too thin, too short here or too long there, because they have this or that skin colour. All human beings should in principle have an equal right to acceptance and respect, regardless of the shape of their body. Racial discrimination is particularly harmful. Skin after all is just skin, whatever its colour. It carries no implication whatsoever about the person itself. It has no relation to whether the person is intelligent or not, honest or not.

SENSUALITY

Racial discrimination is not the only issue. Sexual desire can get really out of hand and lead to horrible things, such as rape, child pornography, and so on. These examples should make it clear that sexual desire cannot simply be equated with love. Rape, for example, is quite definitely not a form of love. On the contrary, it is a dangerous form of mental sickness that brutally inflicts incredible harm. There are times when the rapist even kills the victim. This is the very opposite of love.

Even apart from such extreme manifestations of sensual desire, it seems quite meaningful to be able to curtail or eliminate sexual desire when it occurs in inappropriate situations. Someone might experience the arising of sensual desire towards the partner of their best friend, for example. It would be useful in such a case to be able to quench the flame of lust at the beginning, when doing so is still manageable. If not reined in, the small flame can become a fully fledged fire that burns us and others. Here just reminding ourselves that the body is a combination of anatomical parts can help to get a reality check, to distinguish what is really there from what the mind has made out of it.

The disadvantages of sensual desire find illustration in several similes in the *Potaliya-sutta* (MN 54; Anālayo 2013: 74ff). One simile likens indulging in sensuality to carrying a burning torch against the wind, with the result that the carrier will get burned. Indulging in sensuality is like unskilfully taking hold of a burning torch in such a way that we get burned ourselves. The issue is not the search for pleasure as such; in effect the simile does not imply that there is something wrong in principle with using a torch. The problem is holding the torch in the wrong direction. Applied to the quest for pleasure, the problem is similarly the wrong direction, namely by way of sensual indulgence.

The fire imagery also comes up in the *Māgandiya-sutta* (MN 75; Anālayo 2013: 73). This discourse describes a leper who cauterizes his wounds over a fire. Even though such cauterization will give him temporary relief, it worsens his condition. The same holds for sensuality. The more we indulge in it, the stronger sensual desire will become. In contrast, a healed leper will no longer want to go anywhere near the fire. He would even resist with all his might if he were forcefully dragged to the fire. This illustrates one who has left the fire of sensual desire behind for good. Such a one will not want to be anywhere near indulgence in sensuality, simply because sensual pleasures have completely lost all their former attraction.

Another simile in the *Potaliya-sutta* depicts a hungry dog chewing on a bone, unable to satisfy its hunger. Sensual indulgence similarly is incapable of yielding lasting satisfaction. Just as the taste of the bone seems promising to the dog, so too the pursuit of sensuality seems promising. Yet both fail to live up to their promise.

Still another simile in the same discourse describes a bird that has got hold of a piece of meat and is pursued by other birds trying to get that piece of meat. Unless the bird lets go of the piece of meat, it risks being hurt or even killed by the other birds. This simile illustrates the competition among those who are in quest of sensual gratification. We might think of two men in love with the same woman who may even go so far as to kill each other.

Sensual attraction is closely related to our own sense of identity. This comes to the fore in a discourse in the *Aṅguttara-nikāya* (AN 7.48; Anālayo 2013: 71). The discourse describes how a male tends to identify with his sense of masculinity and find joy in it, just as a female tends to identify with her sense of femininity and find joy in it. Having identified with masculinity within, the man seeks femininity outside, just as the woman, having identified with femininity within, seeks masculinity outside. In this way, yearning for sexual union prevents them from transcending the narrow confines of their sense of identity. Although not explicitly mentioned, the presentation in this discourse could also be applied to the case of same-sex sensual desires. The basic principle remains that letting go of a limited and limiting sense of identity, which is what fuels sensual desire, opens up the path to freedom.

The present exercise offers a training to reach such freedom. It involves a shift of perception away from the default notion of the human body as sexually attractive, in which our society has amply trained us. Think of all the time and resources invested in beautifying and adorning the body. This is such a waste of time and resources, which could be used for better purposes. All that is required is to emerge from the obsession with the body as sexually alluring. Just keeping the body clean and in working order is so much more simple and appropriate.

Strictly speaking, sensual desire falls under the header of the five hindrances. Nevertheless, it might be worth pointing out already here that desire as such is not necessarily a hindrance. The desire to develop ourselves and to progress on the path is certainly praiseworthy. There is no question about this. The problem with sensual types of desire is simply the mistaken belief that true happiness can be found by gratifying the senses. With progress in practice it becomes increasingly clear that it is more worthwhile to cultivate the mind in such a way that it gives rise to wholesome joy and happiness. The joy and happiness experienced during deepening concentration or insight are rooted in a condition of the mind that is aloof from sensual desire. The primary function of the present exercise is to facilitate such seclusion. It is a medicine, a cure to enable the experience of a greater and more refined happiness than we could ever achieve through sensual indulgence. In a way it offers a shift towards developing intimacy within, rather than embarking on the quest for intimacy through external sexual union.

THE SIMILE

As already mentioned in the previous section, the actual contemplation of the anatomical parts as impure or dirty, or as bereft of beauty, is not a form of mindfulness in itself. Instead it is an "examination". This difference needs to be kept in mind. The evaluative element introduced with this examination is not a form of mindfulness itself; it is a practice that is meant to lead to establishing the balanced stance of mindfulness.

The topic of balance and freedom from desire and aversion comes to the fore in the simile that accompanies the present exercise in the *Satipaṭṭhāna-sutta*:

> It is just as a man with good eyes who has opened a double-mouthed bag full of different sorts of grain, such as hill rice, red rice, beans, peas, millet, and white rice, which he would examine: "This is hill rice, this is red rice, these are beans, these are peas, this is millet, and this is white rice."

Looking at various grains in such a bag, apparently used for sowing, would hardly provoke a reaction. We would not think of rice or beans as sexy or want to devise ways of beautifying them. They are simply rice or beans.

The aim of this exercise is to cultivate a similar attitude towards different parts of the body. In effect the list of anatomical parts includes aspects of the human body that are generally considered attractive, such as hair, nails, teeth, and skin. Alongside these come parts that are generally considered as disgusting, such as faeces, bile, phlegm, pus, blood, and so on. In the *Madhyama-āgama* parallel to the *Satipaṭṭhāna-sutta* the instruction is to contemplate the body "according to what is attractive and what is repulsive", thereby explicitly noting that the listing of anatomical parts comprises both aspects (Anālayo 2013: 63). The task is to emerge from attraction and from disgust, learning to perceive the parts of the body with the same attitude that we would have when looking at various grains.

This contemplation could be combined with an acknowledgement of each part's functionality. Such an aspect of practice is mentioned explicitly in the *Ekottarika-āgama* parallel to the *Satipaṭṭhāna-sutta*, which introduces the list of anatomical parts by encouraging contemplation of "this body according to its nature and functions, from head to feet and from feet to head" (Anālayo 2013: 64). It is indeed important to have a functioning human body in order to be able to practise the path. This is worth keeping in mind, as developing aversion towards the body or not taking proper care of it when it is sick can also become an obstacle to progress towards liberation, just as is the case for sensual indulgence.

A PRACTICAL SIMPLIFICATION

For actual practice of this exercise I would like to introduce a simplification. This simplification involves summarizing the different anatomical parts under three headings. These are skin, flesh, and bones. The idea for such a simplification came to me from the *Sampasādanīya-sutta* (DN 28; Anālayo 2013: 72). The relevant passage describes a progression from contemplation of the anatomical parts to being aware just of the bones, leaving aside skin and flesh. This implies that the list of anatomical parts can be summarized under these three aspects. The simplification I am proposing here is just meant as a starting point, leaving it open to each practitioner to change to a more detailed contemplation later on.

The mode of practice I recommend to get started takes the form of body scans. One body scan to become aware of the skin, another to become aware of the flesh, and a third to become aware of the bones.

By way of background to the scans, I would like to say a few words about the relationship between a map and reality in meditation. Our meditative experience is conditioned by both. The teachings passed on by oral transmission are maps to be used for practice. The application of these maps to the reality experienced in meditation becomes mental cultivation (*bhāvanā*). Maps are clearly important, but they are only tools. They are similar to a raft, which is useful for crossing over but afterwards can be discarded. The use of a map as such is not problematic, as long as we make sure beforehand that this map accords with reality. In other words, using a map does not mean giving free rein to any type of imagination. Instead, we make sure that our map is in accordance with reality. Such a map has the potential to lead to knowledge and vision of things as they really are (*yathābhūta*).

Using concepts as aids for the cultivation of insight works well as long as our overall map is in accordance with reality. It not only works well; concepts are actually required. Without the use of any concept, we would hardly be able to know that there are "skin", "flesh", and "bones". We would not even be able to know that "there is a body."

Regarding the correctness of the map, the fact that the human body has the anatomical parts listed in the instructions is beyond doubt. The same holds for the proposition that the body has skin, flesh, and bones. There can hardly be any question about the accuracy of this particular map inasmuch as just the anatomical parts are concerned, leaving aside for the time being the evaluation of these as impure.

When doing a body scan with attention given to skin, flesh, or bones, it is not essential to be able to sense each and every part distinctly. As a matter of fact, the listing in the *Satipaṭṭhāna-sutta* is not comprehensive. Elsewhere the discourses reflect awareness of the brain, for example, which is not mentioned in the instruction for contemplating the body's anatomical parts. Only with later tradition does the brain come to be added to the list (Anālayo 2003: 147n119, 2013: 67, and 2018c: 152).

Whatever anatomical parts are selected for contemplation, we already know that these are in the body. So there is no need to conduct a personal research project aimed at proving their existence and certifying our map. Rather, we are just trying to cultivate a general sense of the constitution of our body. Just knowing that this body is made up of skin (including hairs and nails), of flesh (comprising muscles, tendons, and organs), and of bones (covering also the teeth) is enough.

By way of preparation, we could simply touch our face with the hands to get a feel for skin. Then we could touch the gums with our tongue and get a sense of flesh. Next we could move the lower jaw from one side to the other and forward and backward to get a sense of bones. This much should be within the reach of personal experience for each of us.

Just this much is enough as a starting point. During the actual scanning of the body we might at times have an actual sense of the physical location of some of its parts; we might feel them. But even without a distinct feel, it suffices just to know that they are there. The purpose of the exercise is served by just knowing, without needing to strain ourselves to get a distinct feel.

For the actual scan I suggest starting with the head and moving down to the feet for contemplating the skin. For the flesh I suggest moving up from the feet to the head, and again from the head down to the feet for the bones. This is just one way to do it and practitioners should feel free to change and adjust according to personal preference (an alternative for those who are not comfortable with the scanning method at all would be, for example, to direct awareness to the entirety of the skin, then of the flesh, and then of the bones of the whole body).

During each scan, even though there is a clear focus on either skin, flesh, or bones, it would be ideal if such focus came together with a general sense of the presence of the whole body. The three scans for skin, flesh, and bones involve a progression from the more external to the more internal. This gradually builds up a more three-dimensional apperception of our own body as a whole. Such three-dimensionality in turn provides a firm spatial grounding in whole-body awareness as a tool for the maintenance of present-moment awareness.

A DETAILED APPROACH

Based on sufficient familiarity with this simplified approach of taking up just skin, flesh, and bones as a starter for this exercise, a detailed scan could be developed that takes into account all of the items mentioned in the discourse. In what follows I present one way in which this could take place. Due to being combined with the scan, the order of organs differs from the list in the *Satipaṭṭhāna-sutta*.

When doing the first scan we become aware first of the *head hairs* and then turn to the *skin* in the head area. Attention given to the skin in the face area can be accompanied by noting the *grease* that lubricates the skin in general, together with the occasional manifestation of *pus*, evident in the formation of pimples, such as on the forehead or cheeks. Coming to the eyes in particular can serve as an occasion for noting *tears*, the nostrils for noting *snot*, and the mouth for noting *spittle*. Moving further down, awareness can turn to *body hairs*, which are especially prominent in the armpits, as well as later on when reaching the genital area. The same locations can also be employed for attending to *sweat* as manifesting with particular prominence in the arm pits and genital area, in the awareness that perspiration of course takes

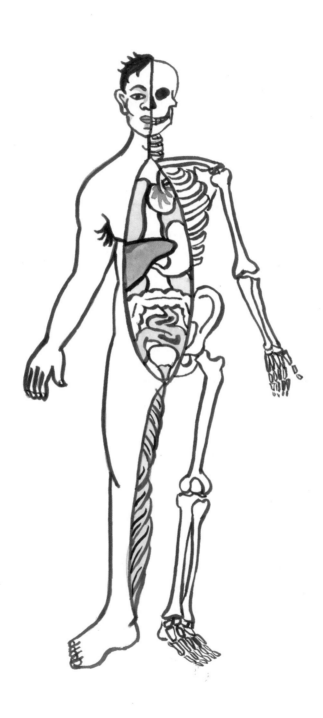

place through the pores of the skin of the whole body. When coming to the skin of the hands and later of the feet the *nails* can be noted. When reaching the buttocks, attention given to the skin can come in conjunction with noting subcutaneous *fat*.

During the second scan, from the feet onwards awareness of *flesh* can be combined with noting also the *sinews*. These are in fact quite evident right away when starting with the feet. On reaching the genital area, the bladder containing *urine* and the *bowels* containing *faeces* can come in for specific attention. Contemplation could proceed by turning to the *mesentery*, the *kidneys*, the *spleen*, the *contents of the stomach*, and the *liver* with its *bile*. Next come the *diaphragm* and the *lungs*, which can be related to the manifestation of *phlegm*. Turning to the *heart* can come in conjunction with noting the *blood* that the heart pumps throughout the body. Contemplation continues with the fleshy parts and the sinews in the arms as well as in the head.

The third scan could begin with the *bones* of the skull and the *teeth*, and then move on to the bones and the *bone-marrow* of the remainder of the skeleton. When coming to a joint between two bones, the *oil of the joints* could also be noted.

This is just one possible way a detailed scan could be carried out, based on the anatomical parts listed in the instructions, albeit in a different sequence. Perhaps this suggestion could serve as a starting point for each practitioner to develop a mode of contemplation that best suits individual needs and preferences. In general, however, my recommendation is to begin by at first just using skin, flesh, and bones. That much suffices for progressing to the goal of the practice.

KEEPING AN EYE ON BALANCE

As far as the evaluation is concerned, the question of whether the body is indeed impure, dirty, or not beautiful is not as self-evident and acceptable for many practitioners as the fact that it is made up of these various anatomical parts. Whereas a map based on these parts can hardly be put into question, whether the evaluation should become part of the map used for practice depends on our personal assessment. Therefore I would leave it up to each practitioner to decide to what extent an element of evaluation feels appropriate. Although for monastics dedicated to a life of celibacy a strong version of the evaluative element would be quite appropriate, the same is not necessarily the case for a lay practitioner living the family life. Yet, according to the discourses, several lay disciples were accomplished practitioners of *satipaṭṭhāna* (Anālayo 2003: 275). In view of the diversity of situations from which practitioners can come, it seems best to allow for different modalities of the present exercise.

An important starting point for this practice is mindful recognition of the type of relationship we have towards our own body. If this relationship is one of aversion towards the body, it is important to avoid doing anything that further strengthens such aversion. If we already tend to feel frustrated or even depressed because our body does not meet current standards of physical beauty and attractiveness, it would be unwise to employ the evaluation. Instead we might turn attention just to the fact that the body is made up of skin, flesh, and bones, which perform their function independent of what society considers to be good looks. So the apposite approach would be to do the scan just to arouse an attitude of balance, similar to looking at various grains. A reflection along the lines of non-attachment will be appropriate, especially for practitioners who are negatively disposed towards their own body. After all, it is just skin, flesh, and bones.

There is no problem in deciding to go for this option. On the contrary, it is an essential part of proper mindfulness practice to recognize clearly where we are and where we want to go. Such mindful monitoring can lead to the realization that the evaluative element does not fit our present situation. The type of *satipaṭṭhāna* meditation I am presenting here covers three different body contemplations. This leaves room for each practitioner to choose which of these three should be given more emphasis. It is perfectly fine to approach this particular body contemplation softly. There is no need to force ourselves to do something that turns out not to be beneficial.

The same holds even more if we are the victim of abuse or of other body-related traumas. In such a case we first of all need to find a way of inhabiting the body without giving rise to negativity. The employment of an evaluation that increases negativity would be counterproductive and could even be damaging. In such a situation it is appropriate to opt just for the simple practice of being aware of skin, flesh, and bones, together with a continuous monitoring of how this affects our present relationship to the body. Based on such continuous assessment through mindfulness, we will then be able to decide how to proceed.

At times even skin, flesh, and bones may be too much and it might be best to start just with the bones, being aware of the skeleton only, as this is an area that is usually not emotionally charged and at the same time allows us to centre ourselves and inhabit the body. Alternatively it could also be an option to work just with a part of the body that feels safe. This could be, for example, the feet. So we just direct attention to that part of the body for the scans and only gradually and softly expand to other parts of the body, inasmuch as and only to the extent that these also begin to feel safe.

The overall aim of the practice it to arrive at a balanced and healthy attitude towards the body, an attitude that is just as much free from sensual desire as it is free from aversion or disgust. Therefore the degree to which an element of evaluation is brought in depends on mindfully monitoring where we are at present and what is required in order to foster balance.

Based on such an assessment, some of us might feel ready to confront a tendency to sensual obsession in relation to the body. In such a case, it would be appropriate to bring in the element of evaluation. We might decide to use the terminology found in the discourse, "impure" or "dirty", or else "not sexually attractive". For those who wish to go even further, here I offer some additional suggestions. But it should be clear that these are only meant for those who really want to confront sexual desire head-on. The same also holds for reading the next two paragraphs, which some readers might prefer to skip.

A way of strengthening the impact of such practice is to keep in mind, during the first scan concerned with the skin, that the outer skin is dead matter. The outer part of the skin is made up of dead cells which keep flaking off. The body exudes grease which keeps the dead cells in place. This mixture of dead skin cells and grease attracts bacteria. Every square centimetre of our skin is a feeding ground for millions of bacteria. Just below this feeding ground for bacteria, as soon as things become alive, it gets bloody right away.

Another way of strengthening the impact of this meditation could be by introducing an exercise found in the *Ekottarika-āgama* parallel to the *Satipaṭṭhāna-sutta* and also in a Pāli discourse (AN 9.15; Anālayo 2013: 40f). This exercise draws attention to the dirty liquids that come out of the nine orifices of the body. The nine orifices are the eyes, the ears, the nostrils, the mouth, the urethra, and the anus. The eyes discharge mucus, the ears wax, the nostrils snot, the mouth bile and phlegm, the urethra urine, and the anus faeces. During the scan, when passing each orifice, we can for a moment become aware of its specific discharge. This mode of practice has some overlap with the detailed approach described earlier. It differs in so far as it involves attending specifically to liquids exuded by the body.

Whichever of these modes of practice we feel more comfortable with, it is of crucial importance that it leads to balance. A discourse in the *Saṃyutta-nikāya* reports an episode where a group of monastics overdid this exercise. Having engaged in this type of practice without wisdom and a proper understanding of its purpose, they cultivated disgust with their own bodies to the extent that several of them committed suicide (SN 54.9). Elsewhere I have studied this episode in detail, finding that the Pāli account shows signs of later expansion and exaggeration (Anālayo 2014b). Leaving aside apparent exaggerations, however, the story as such still serves as a strong warning. This type of practice should never be allowed to unbalance the mind. In this way, already the first of the body contemplations requires paying some attention to the condition of our own mind, a topic that will become particularly prominent with the third *satipaṭṭhāna*.

Maintaining balance is central for all *satipaṭṭhāna* meditation. The task of mindfulness is precisely to supervise and monitor how the practice affects us. If we turn a blind eye to negative repercussions of our meditation practice, then this is actually a loss of mindfulness. In a way we miss a main point of *satipaṭṭhāna* practice. Should contemplation of the anatomical parts lead to negativity or a sense of aversion towards the body, the presence of mindfulness can immediately alert us to the loss of balance. We then counterbalance by shifting to mindfulness of the body as our good friend, letting go of any form of evaluation we have been using at this point. In this way, we gradually learn to dwell independently without clinging to anything.

Another dimension of balancing out the practice relates to its internal and external application. Contemplation of the anatomical parts starts off with our own body. Once this has been well developed, the basic understanding gained in this way (combined with whatever evaluation we have decided to adopt) can then be applied to the bodies of others. This eventually leads to a comprehensive understanding of the nature of the human body, be it our own or that of others.

FROM SCANNING TO OPEN PRACTICE

Besides serving as a basis for whatever mode of evaluation we might decide to adopt, gradual scanning through the body has the function of collecting the mind. It is particularly helpful when the mind is distracted. The step-by-step procedure of moving in sequence from one part of the body to the next helps to keep the mind engaged with the meditation practice. It also makes it easy to notice when the mind has wandered away. We might start with the head, move on to the neck, and all of a sudden find we have already reached the feet. Something has gone missing. Due to the sequential procedure of the scan, it becomes easier to notice when the mind has wandered off.

At first it would be helpful to do these scans slowly in order to grow accustomed to this type of practice. But with growing familiarity they can at times be done more quickly. In the beginning we might take up arms and legs singly, but later the two arms or the two legs can be done simultaneously. Needless to say, the foregoing is not meant to imply that quick scanning is a marker of proficiency. Even after much practice of this exercise, chances are that we will still find slow scanning to be beneficial, simply because it allows the mind to savour more fully the contemplation. In the end it all depends on our present state of mind and preference. Recognizing the most appropriate way to practise at any given moment is the task of mindfulness and clearly knowing.

Genuine *satipaṭṭhāna* meditation is not about stoically repeating the same thing over and over again, to the extent that the mind just becomes dull. Instead, it requires constant alertness to the condition of our mind. How is the mind right now? What does it require?

When the mind tends to distraction, it might be best to proceed slowly and in much detail when doing the scan. When the mind is collected, it might be better to move more quickly. It is not the case that there is one right way of practising that is applicable at all times. Rather, the right way of contemplating comes about by clearly understanding what is required at any given moment.

Having done the scans, whether slow or fast, we move on to just being aware of the body in the sitting posture as made up of skin, flesh, and bones. With the continuity of our attitude of non-attachment we become ready to open up to just being aware of the present moment in whatever way it unfolds. Having stabilized the mind through the scans and introduced a healthy dose of non-attachment, we move on to an undirected mode of practice. Mindfulness is firmly rooted in the body and we stay receptively open to whatever manifests with any of the senses. We are fully present and aware of anything that manifests, aware of it as a changing phenomenon. This is what constitutes the difference from the cowherd's mindfulness: recognition of impermanence. This holds for the body whose anatomical constitution keeps changing all the time. It holds as well for anything we experience; whatever happens is a process, a flow, a flux. Aware of change in all dimensions of our experience, we are planting seeds of wisdom and insight that will ripen in liberation from all sensuality and unwholesome states.

Whenever distractions occur, as soon as we recognize that this has happened, smilingly we come back to the present moment.

With shorter distractions we just come back to resting in open awareness in the here and now, coming back to the presence of our good friend *sati*. She is always there, ready to be with us. In the case of longer distractions, it might be opportune to take up the body scans again. Proceeding once more through skin, flesh, and bones will help to regain the continuity of mindfulness.

When the time has come to move on to walking meditation, the same knowing of the body as made up of skin, flesh, and bones can continue. This is similar to the awareness of the whole body in the sitting posture after the completion of the three scans. From skin, flesh, and bones seated we proceed to skin, flesh, and bones walking or else just the bones walking. Based on attending to aspects of the walking body, walking meditation can lead to a general sense of the whole body combined with an opening of awareness to whatever manifests at any sense-door. The gist of contemplation of the anatomical parts is to inculcate an attitude of non-attachment towards the body and to cultivate a rootedness of mindfulness in the body. The same attitude and rootedness can carry over from sitting to walking and eventually to any activity to be performed.

In the simile of the wheel that I like to use to illustrate this approach to *satipaṭṭhāna* meditation, the first spoke of contemplating the anatomical parts makes distinct contributions to both the hub and the outer rim. The contribution made to the hub of mindfulness of the body is that, owing to the gradual scanning through different parts of the body in sequential order, we develop a distinctly felt sense of the body as a whole. This serves to root mindfulness more firmly in the body. The contribution to the outer rim of dwelling independently without clinging to anything lies in the cultivation of non-attachment towards the body's external appearance.

SUMMARY

Contemplation of the anatomical constitution of the body comes with an evaluative element that needs to be carefully adjusted to our personal situation and needs. The main thrust of the exercise is towards engendering non-attachment, such that different parts of the body can be regarded with the same attitude we would have when looking at various grains. For practical purposes, the listing of anatomical parts can be simplified by employing just the three categories of skin, flesh, and bones. These can be explored with the help of body scanning, which at the same time serves to root mindfulness firmly in the body.

IV

ELEMENTS

Contemplation of the four elements is the second spoke in the wheel of practice I am presenting here. Here are the relevant instructions from the *Satipaṭṭhāna-sutta* (MN 10):

> One examines this same body, however it is placed, however disposed, by way of the elements: "In this body there are the earth element, the water element, the fire element, and the wind element."

THE ELEMENTS AS QUALITIES

In early Buddhist thought the elements represent qualities. A discourse in the *Aṅguttara-nikāya* describes how a skilled practitioner can consider a tree as a manifestation of each of the four elements (AN 6.41; Anālayo 2003: 150n138). However solid it appears, a tree is not only a manifestation of the earth element. It can similarly be seen as a manifestation of the water element, the fire element, or the wind element. The reason is that each of these qualities is present in a tree. Besides the wood, there is sap and temperature in the tree, and motion takes place inside of it. This illustrates the orientation of the early Buddhist analysis of matter into elements, which concerns mere qualities; it does not posit a form of essentialism or atomism.

As qualities, the earth element represents the principles of hardness, resistance, and stiffness, the water element liquidity, wetness, and cohesion, the fire element the domain of temperature, manifesting as different degrees of warmth and heat, and the wind element the principle of motion, vibration, and oscillation.

To gain a sense of each of these elements, we could grit our teeth to get a feel for hardness as a manifestation of the earth element. The earth element is found throughout the whole body, but it is particularly evident in the bones. Next we could gather the spittle in our mouth and swallow it. Then we notice how the dryness in our mouth is gradually being replaced by wetness as spittle again accumulates in the mouth. The water element is found throughout the body, but it is particularly evident in the various bodily liquids. Rubbing our hands together we can feel heat. The fire element is found throughout the body, but it is particularly evident on the skin level. Taking a deep breath, we are aware of the motion of oxygen. The wind element is found throughout the body, but it is particularly evident in the constant motion of breath moving in and out of the body.

According to later tradition, the water element cannot be experienced directly. Although an adult human body consists of up to 60 per cent of water, this is indeed the one out of the four elements that is not easily felt distinctly. However, I would argue that the exercise suggested above regarding spittle shows that it is possible to have a distinct sense of wetness as a manifestation of the water element. The same holds for the felt sense of other bodily liquids, such as sweat, tears, urine, etc. Apart from bodily liquids, another experience that points in the same direction is when we sit on a seat that we did not notice was wet. The wetness gradually penetrates through our clothing until it reaches the skin of our buttocks, at which point we suddenly realize: "Oh no, this is wet!" I take this as a direct experience of the water element.

In a wider sense, the water element stands for the principle of cohesion. This can be related to the formation of hydrogen bonds between molecules. Hydrogen bonds also occur in proteins and DNA. This makes it indeed seem meaningful to view the water element as exemplifying connectedness, the bonding together of things as opposed to their falling apart. Wet clothes stick to the body, wet paper sticks to the wall, and so on.

Similar to the contemplation of the anatomical parts, in the present case it is also not necessary to strain ourselves in order to feel distinctly each and every aspect of the manifestation of the four elements in the body. The map we are using for our practice is in accordance with reality. Matter is indeed made up of some degree of solidity, some degree of cohesion, it has some temperature, and it is in constant motion within. There can hardly be any doubt about the accuracy of this map. Since this map is in accordance with reality, it is not necessary for us to conduct sustained research in order to ascertain the correctness of this map in every single part of our body. It is sufficient, for our present purposes, to combine awareness of the body with the knowledge derived from this map.

Contemplation of the elements could be compared to receiving a parcel meant for someone else. There is no need to open the parcel and search its contents. It is enough to look at the address label, realize that this parcel is not mine, and return it to the postman. The main thrust of contemplation of the elements is to realize that none can truly be considered "mine". Just as we do not need to search through the contents of a parcel that does not belong to us, so it is with the elements. There is no need to search through the whole body for each of them. There is also no need to analyse a particular sensation in an attempt to determine which element this precisely corresponds to. The contemplation is about the four elements as together making up the physical reality of the body, independent of how and in what way their actual interrelation manifests. It is enough for us to know that, however the elements manifest, they are not mine; they are empty of a self. The gist of the practice is simply about no longer taking the body so very personally and learning to relate to it without self-investment.

A PRACTICAL APPROACH

For actual practice I suggest using the same scanning method already employed for the contemplation of the anatomical parts.

Starting with the head we move down to the feet, contemplating the earth element. During this scan we are aware of the whole body pervaded by the earth element, with particular attention given to the skeleton, as this is the most prominent manifestation of the earth element. For the water element I suggest moving up from the feet to the head, and again from the head down to the feet for the fire element, and finally once more from the feet up to the head for the wind element. Each time we are aware of the whole body being pervaded by the respective element.

At the same time, we might note that the water element is particular prominent in the bodily liquids found in the fleshy parts of the body. The fire element is quite evident on the skin level, as this part of the body is specifically sensitive to temperature. The wind element is especially noticeable in the process of breathing.

As we practise in this way, the body scans for the elements build on the scanning done for the anatomical parts. To some degree the elements earth, water, and fire correspond to the earlier distinction of the body's anatomy into bones, flesh, and skin. A difference is that during the earlier practice there was a stronger focus on the bones as standing out prominently against the rest of the whole body. When contemplating the earth element, the bones become a considerably more integral dimension of the whole of the body. The same holds for flesh and skin.

In addition to these three, a new aspect of practice enters the scene with the wind element, representing any motion of or in the body. Motion manifests with particular prominence in the breath. Just as skin, flesh, and bones in a way build a bridge from the anatomical parts to the elements, so too the breath builds a bridge from the elements to the third body contemplation, to be taken up in the next chapter.

Regarding the experience of the breath, I recommend that each practitioner decide where and in what manner the breath can most readily be felt. Some prefer to note the process of breathing through attending to the sensations below the nostrils and above the upper lip. Others prefer the inside of the nostrils or the back of the throat. Others aim at the movement distinguishable in the chest area or the rise and fall of the abdomen. Still others prefer to be aware of the breath without focusing on a specific location.

For the mode of practice that I present here, it does not matter at all. Whatever works best for us to get a clear sense of the distinction between breathing in and breathing out is the right way to proceed. The only point to be kept in mind is that the breath is best experienced as part of an awareness of the whole body. It should not become the object of an all-out focus on the breath alone.

Besides the process of breathing, the impact of the element wind also becomes apparent when we notice slight motions of various types taking place in the body. On a subtle level the body is in continuous motion, and most of this happens without our conscious intention; in fact usually we do not even notice it. This discovery already serves as a pointer to the main insight dimension of contemplation of elements, which is the empty nature of the body.

When shifting from sitting to walking meditation, the earlier cultivated awareness of skin, flesh, and bones during walking could be continued, viewing each as a prominent exemplification of the first three elements of earth, water, and fire. The fourth element of wind naturally becomes evident in the very fact that the body is now moving rather than stationary.

Whereas contemplation of the anatomical constitution of the body during walking meditation is in particular concerned with non-attachment, with the elements attention instead shifts to the empty nature of the walking experience. We train ourselves to let go of any identification with the walking body. The gist of such practice could be summed up with the injunction: "walk without (any notion of) a walker!"

THE SIMILE

The purpose of contemplation of the elements finds illustration in a simile in the *Satipaṭṭhāna-sutta*, which proceeds as follows:

> It is just as a skilled butcher or a butcher's apprentice who, having killed a cow, were to be seated at a crossroads with it cut up into pieces.

It is remarkable that the rather challenging exercise of deconstructing the notion of bodily beauty through contemplation of the anatomical parts uses the comparably soft illustration of a bag full of grains. In contrast, the present exercise comes with this gruesome depiction of a butchered cow. Given the high regard afforded to cows in ancient India and the emphasis among practitioners like the Jains on not harming any living being, the example seems intentionally shocking.

The implication of this simile becomes particularly evident in the *Ekottarika-āgama* parallel to the *Satipaṭṭhāna-sutta*. This version describes how, once the butcher has cut up the cow, he sees various parts of the cow as: "these are the feet", "this is the heart", "these are the tendons", and "this is the head" (Anālayo 2013: 82). In other words, what earlier for him was a "cow" now has become pieces of meat for sale. The presentation in the

Ekottarika-āgama parallel is in accordance with the understanding in the Pāli commentary (Anālayo 2003: 151).

Just as the butcher cuts up the cow into pieces of meat, in the same way we can butcher up clinging to a sense of selfhood and cut it into pieces. I take it that the strong nuances conveyed by the simile are intended to drive home the need to carry out this practice to its successful completion. Clinging to a solid sense of self is in fact the main culprit responsible for a broad range of problems and afflictions. The task is to leave behind the notion of "my body" as a compact unit that can be owned and that is substantially different from other bodies. Instead, it is to be seen as just a combination of the four elements, similar in this respect to all other manifestations of matter.

THE EMPTY NATURE OF MATTER

All forms of discrimination based on gender or race can be butchered by attending to the elements. We are all composed of these same elements. Once this is realized, material distinctions between human beings are revealed to lack any true substance. According to quantum physics, this body is for the most part just empty space. The physical difference between the beautiful young model on stage and the old beggar by the side of the road is so minimal as to be negligible. How could such a difference be truly significant? What basis do we really have for identifying ourselves as a member of a particular group with certain physical marks considered to be fundamentally different from another group with other physical characteristics?

It is not only alleged differences between human beings that can be butchered with this exercise. The whole material world is made up of these four elements. Whether inside this body or outside of it, there is just earth, water, fire, and wind. The gradual diminishing of the assumption of a substantial difference between manifestations of these elements internally as "me" and externally as "others" undermines the very foundation on which craving and attachment rely.

The *Mahāhatthipadopama-sutta* relates the four internal elements to their external counterparts found outside in nature (MN 28; Anālayo 2003: 152). Both internal and external manifestations of the elements are similarly impermanent. They share being subject to the same law of change. This puts an additional spotlight on impermanence.

Contemplation of the elements can naturally lead from internal elements within the body to external manifestations of the elements outside of the body, culminating in an appreciation of their impermanent nature. Having proceeded from the head to the feet, experiencing the hardness of the earth element internally, we could for a moment sense the hardness of the ground on which we sit as an exemplification of the hardness of all matter around us. In preparation for the next scan we might notice the lack of separation between the meditation seat and our buttocks. Although in this case the lack of separation is because of the pressure of the weight of the body, the sense of connectedness to the meditation mat requires the cohesion of the water element in those bodily parts that touch the meditation mat. Therefore it does seem possible to take this physically felt connectedness to the ground as an exemplification of the cohesion responsible for the material particles of this body not just falling apart into disconnected specks of dust.

Beginning the scan for the fire element we might briefly attend to the sensed feeling of the outside temperature around the head area (or just the face if the head is covered by clothing), before moving on to experiencing manifestations of the fire element within the body. With the wind element we could broaden our perspective from experiencing the breath inside the body to noting how air comes from the outside and on exhalation returns to the outside. The suggestion here is not meant to encourage following the breath as it leaves the body, but only to broaden our perspective so that the external dimension is encompassed as well.

By attending briefly to these external dimensions without allowing them to distract us from the actual practice of being in the body, the interdependence between the body and outside nature becomes more a matter of personal experience. The narrow sense of selfhood can be allowed to dissolve in the vastness of nature around us. In a way looking at nature externally can seem as if we are looking in a mirror. All that is there internally and externally is just the elements. We learn to overcome the limitations of our confined sense of bodily identity by becoming part of something larger. The body is just part of nature; it is made up of these four elements just like the rest of nature outside. This body does not really belong to us; it belongs to nature, it has been borrowed from nature, and it will eventually return to nature when the four elements fall apart at the time of death.

Our existence is entirely dependent on the outside world, and both are merely changing processes. The division we tend to create between the elements in this body as something "I am" and manifestations of the elements outside of this body as something substantially different from what "I am" is being put into question. At what point exactly does it feel right to consider food to have become "my body": is it when I have it on my spoon, in my mouth, when I chew, or when I swallow it? At what point does it lose the right to this qualification: when it leaves the stomach, when it proceeds from the small to the large intestine, or only when it is excreted?

Moreover, the assumption to believe we are in control, evident in the tendency to seek to own material things, is similarly being questioned. In truth and fact, the elements are not something we can fully control or permanently own.

The sense of being different from outside nature, in combination with the conceit of ownership and control, is the chief culprit for many a problem. The destruction of the natural environment, pollution, and climate change have acquired dimensions that threaten the very survival of the human race. It is high time for us to realize that we cannot continue to live in this way. Contemplation of the elements can make a substantial contribution towards deepening this realization. The elements inside and the elements outside are not different in principle. They are part of one single continuity. It is our responsibility to take care of nature outside just as much as we take care of our own body.

Contemplation of the elements offers a convenient entrance into what could be considered the most central dimension of insight in early Buddhist thought: not-self (*anattā*). The same could alternatively be captured with the term "empty", in the sense that everything is empty of a self. The term "self" in such contexts can be misunderstood. The statement that there is no self does not mean that there is nothing at all. "Self" here refers to a permanent and substantial entity, something that is able to exert complete control. Such an entity cannot be found in any aspect of experience. This is what emptiness in early Buddhism is about. Actually emptiness in early Buddhism is about being empty of something. The body is empty of a permanent self that is in control. That is precisely why the body is not always the way we want it to be, why it becomes sick and eventually passes away.

The denial of a permanent and self-sufficient entity differs from the use of a term like "oneself". This can be clarified with contemplation of the four elements. We know from quantum physics that matter is ultimately just energy processes interacting with one another in a large amount of space. There is nothing substantial or permanent. Everything is just a constant flow and flux under the influence of causes and conditions. Yet this does not mean that we can just walk through a wall. The wall is definitely there right in front of us and, no matter how thoroughly we have studied quantum physics, if we try to walk through it, we will bang our head.

The teaching on emptiness or not-self is similar. It certainly does not deny the subjective sense of continuity or the influence of karma. The point is only that such continuity is not due to some solid, unchanging, and substantial core within ourselves. Instead, it is due to a process of causes and conditions. The other side of the coin of emptiness is conditionality. In other words, the apparent void of emptiness is filled by causes and conditions.

This in turn relates to the fact that there is no mono-causality to be found anywhere. Whatever there is, it results from an interplay of a range of causes and conditions. Some of these causes and conditions fall within the sphere of our influence. Others operate outside of it. We can influence things, but we are not in full control.

Staying just within the confines of a single life, it should be obvious that what we have done in the past influences what we are at present. What we learned at school and later is what enables us now to perform the tasks in which we are engaged. The earlier learning is our "karmic deed" and our present abilities are its "karmic fruit".

As a general pattern, selfishness and cruelty lead to suffering, just as kindness and generosity lead to happiness. Results do not invariably manifest right on the spot, just as a single day of learning at school does not immediately result in getting a job. In effect not everything learned at school will be of future use. Nevertheless, there is a general tendency for learning and study to lead to better employment. Again, not every act of selfishness and cruelty will immediately issue in suffering, and not every instance of kindness and generosity yields instant happiness. Still there is a general tendency for selfishness and cruelty to have negative results for ourselves and others, just as kindness and generosity tend to have positive results. None of this conflicts with the teaching on not-self or emptiness, just as quantum physics does not conflict with the experience of the solidity of walls.

Not only is there no conflict, but the teaching on emptiness even has a direct relevance to the contrast between cruelty and kindness. Cruelty and a whole range of unwholesome reactions have their foundation in selfishness. To the degree to which insight into emptiness is able to deconstruct selfishness, to that degree mental space opens up for the growth of kindness and other wholesome mental attitudes. Just as conditionality is the other side of the coin of emptiness from a functional perspective, so from an affective perspective the *brahmavihāras* are the natural flourishing that emerges once a diminishing of egoism has been brought about through insight into emptiness.

This in turn goes to show that emptiness does not make us dysfunctional. On the contrary, to the extent to which we are able to let go of the burden of ego and self-reference, to that extent we become more functional and better at doing what we have to do. In this way, cultivating insight into emptiness is quite different from a tendency to dissociate and become disconnected. It is the precise opposite of that. Just as equanimity is poles apart from indifference, similarly genuine insight into emptiness is far away from escapism.

Due to the emphasis given throughout the practice to an embodied form of mindfulness as the central reference point, helpful groundwork has been established to counter any tendency to dissociation. If such a tendency should manifest, then this calls for increased emphasis on embodied presence of the mind. This will ensure that the type of emptiness cultivated is a genuine one, which will manifest through the natural flourishing of the *brahmavihāras*.

During actual contemplation of the elements, the fact of conditionality can be practically explored in terms of the dependence of our own body on the elements outside. This body is entirely dependent on an adequate supply of the four elements from outside. It can survive without receiving supplies of the earth element in the form of food for a few months at most. Our body can survive without being supplied with the water element in the form of beverages for just some days. It can survive being deprived of the fire element in the form of warmth, such as when naked outside in cold winter, only for hours. It can survive without supply of the wind element in the form of oxygen merely for minutes. Our body is entirely dependent on these four elements. Out of these four, the one element we most pressingly need is at the same time the most ephemeral of the four: the wind element in the form of the motion of air going in and out. This dependency reveals the precariousness of our physical existence.

Such precariousness is not something that affects only ourselves. It is a predicament we share with all other living beings. In this way a realization of emptiness and conditionality is naturally accompanied by an opening of the heart to compassion.

THE ELEMENTS AND MENTAL BALANCE

A discourse in the *Aṅguttara-nikāya* relates the elements to the mental balance of a fully awakened one (AN 9.11; Anālayo 2013: 94f). The arahant Sāriputta had been falsely accused by another monastic. In order to clear up the false allegation, Sāriputta described his mental attitude, thereby implicitly assuring others that he was incapable of doing what he had been accused of. This description compares his mental attitude to the earth. Just as the earth does not react with disgust when something dirty is thrown on it, so too the mind of an arahant cannot react with anger and aversion. Again, water does not react if something dirty is thrown into it. Fire does not react when something disgusting is burned in it. Wind does not react to the repulsiveness of things on which it blows. Whatever happens, the elements do not take it personally. In the same way, the mind of an arahant is free from aversion and irritation; it does not take things personally.

This episode invites us to use the natural manifestations of the elements outside in nature as an exemplification of stability of the mind within. In this way, recollecting the elements can be used as an inspiration to cultivate the absence of reactivity that is characteristic of those who have walked the path all the way to its completion.

A similar perspective emerges from the *Mahārāhulovādasutta* (MN 62; Anālayo 2003: 152). The instructions given in this discourse begin by describing the elements, with the element earth and the element water covering the same anatomical parts that are also listed in the exercise taken up in the previous chapter. The two elements of fire and wind find exemplification in various manifestations of heat and motion respectively. In addition to these four elements, the discourse also brings in the element of space. In each case the task is to proceed from a recognition of the internal manifestations of any element to an awareness of its external manifestations outside in nature. In order to cultivate dispassion with each element, the final instruction is invariably that the element should be contemplated as not being me or mine.

The discourse goes on to describe a mode of meditation that resembles the attitude of the arahant Sāriputta in the passage mentioned earlier. The recommendation is to cultivate a state of mind like the earth, which does not react with disgust when something dirty is thrown on it. As we practise in this way, the dichotomy of pleasure and pain will no longer be able to overwhelm the mind. The instructions continue for the elements of water, fire, and wind in the same manner. In each case a state of mind should be cultivated that resembles the respective element, as a result of which pleasure and pain will no longer overwhelm the mind.

The element earth can also be used to exemplify our rootedness in what is wholesome and productive of welfare for ourselves and others. Again, similar to water, which adapts its form to wherever it flows, so we can train ourselves to be flexible and adaptive to outer circumstances. Just as fire provides warmth to those who are shivering with cold, so we can offer the warmth of our heart to the lonely and desolate. Comparable to wind that keeps moving, in the same way we keep progressing on the path to liberation. In this or any other way, the four elements can be employed as metaphors for mental qualities to be cultivated.

THE ELEMENT SPACE

Lastly in the *Mahārāhulovāda-sutta* comes the element space. Here it is no longer a question of not reacting to dirty and disgusting things. Instead, the instruction is to develop a mind like space, which is not established anywhere.

The perception of space cultivated in this manner in a way sums up the understanding of emptiness that can be developed with the help of the elements. As mentioned earlier, matter is for the most part just space. Space is always there, in any situation. It just takes a moment of paying attention to notice it. This can be particularly helpful when confronted with strong reactions by others. Whatever dirt may be thrown at us, just a moment of attention given to the space between ourselves and the other(s), and from that to the space all around us, can help to maintain balance of the mind (Anālayo 2017c: 196). Attending to space allows the mind to become spacious and keeps it from contracting and becoming narrow and confined. In a way space simply leaves no solid landing place for the reactions of others or our own reactivity to that. In terms of the challenge posed by the hindrances and other problems, rather than leading to a time- and energy-consuming need to engage in battle, these can just be allowed to dissolve. From the vantage point of that mental space, we are so much better able to deal efficiently with whatever problem has manifested.

Cultivating the perception of space can also be undertaken supported by gradually proceeding through the four elements in the sequence in which they are described in the discourse. On following the mode of contemplation described above, the shift from the earth element to the water element in this body can be accompanied by the recognition that it is because of cohesion that this body does not just crumble to dust. Without the principle of cohesion, the apparently so solid floor on which we sit would be like quicksand. In other words, the earth element depends on the water element; it cannot exist without it. The very quality of solidity depends on the quality of cohesion.

In the case of the transition from water to fire, a similar reflection can be undertaken. For water to perform its cohesive function, it has to be at the right temperature. If it is too cold, water freezes and becomes brittle; if it is too warm, it evaporates. For water to perform its cohesive function in a living body, it is crucial that this body be kept within the appropriate temperature range. Unless this temperature range is maintained, the body will pass away and fall apart. Without the appropriate temperature, the quality of cohesion will not be able to perform its function. In this way the water element in this body depends on the fire element.

Regarding the transition from fire to wind, temperature is simply a result of motion. Without motion, there would not be any manifestation of fire. Motion in turn depends on space. Without space, motion could hardly take place. In this way the four elements can be contemplated as depending on one another in such a way that this leads up to the perception of space.

This mode of practice helps to diminish clinging rapidly. The insubstantial nature of the body becomes a palpable, personal, and direct experience, and the findings of quantum physics, which at first sight might seem far removed from our subjective experience of the body, make increasingly more sense.

OPEN PRACTICE

After having explored the elements through the four scans, we move on to just being aware of the body in the sitting posture as made up of earth, water, fire, and wind. Building on the gradual diminishing of identification with the body, we are ready to open up to being aware of the empty nature of the present moment in whatever way it unfolds. We move on to an undirected mode of practice. Mindfulness remains firmly rooted in the body and we stay widely open to whatever manifests with any of the senses, experienced as changing phenomena. The resultant practice is somewhat like looking at flowing water in a creek or stream. Due to the swift flow of the water, we are not really able to discern minor details. What stands out prominently in our vision is instead the constant flow.

In the case of shorter distractions, comparable to meeting someone on the road and just exchanging greetings, we simply come back to being with our good friend *sati*. In the case of longer distractions, similar to meeting someone on the road and sitting down to have a longer conversation, we can again take up the contemplation of the elements. Before doing that, for a moment we discern the empty nature of whatever thought, memory, or fantasy has caused the distraction. The body made up of the four elements is empty just as the mind caught up in some distraction is empty.

The previous exercise of contemplating the body's anatomy has already imbued our practice with a sense of non-attachment. Building on that, the present exercise instils in us a sense of freedom from identification, from holding on to this body as mine.

In terms of the simile of the wheel that illustrates this approach to *satipaṭṭhāna* meditation, contemplation of the elements continues a task already begun by contemplation of the anatomical parts, which is rooting mindfulness firmly in the body. With contemplation of the elements the process of breathing receives additional attention as part of awareness of the whole of the body. This serves to strengthen further the type of rootedness in whole-body awareness that forms the hub of the wheel of practice. Attending to the process of breathing as an integral part of whole-body awareness offers a convenient reference point for not getting lost and succumbing to distractions when shifting to open awareness. The contribution made by contemplation of the elements to the outer rim is a gradual lessening of identification with the body. This comes together with an increasing appreciation of our connectedness to others and the environment, which in turn naturally gives rise to compassion.

SUMMARY

The four elements of earth, water, fire, and wind represent qualities. These can be experienced with body scans, discerning the presence of solidity, cohesion/wetness, temperature, and motion inside of our body. The main thrust of this contemplation is to gain insight into the empty nature of the body and its intrinsic interrelation with matter outside of it. Such insight into the empty nature of all aspects of material existence can serve as a foundation for an opening of the heart and the establishment of inner balance in the face of any challenge.

V

DEATH

The third spoke in the wheel of practice presented here, and the last of the three body contemplations, takes up the stages of decay through which a corpse would go if it were left out in the open. The instructions in the *Satipaṭṭhāna-sutta* are fairly long, wherefore I here present only an abbreviated version (MN 10):

> As though one were to see a corpse thrown away in a charnel ground that is one, two, or three days dead, being bloated, livid, and oozing matter, and one compares this same body with it: "This body too is of the same nature, it will be like that, it is not exempt from that fate."

> Again as though one were to see a corpse thrown away in a charnel ground that is being devoured by crows, hawks, vultures, dogs, jackals, or various kinds of worms …

> a corpse thrown away in a charnel ground, a skeleton with flesh and blood, held together by the sinews …

> a skeleton without flesh, smeared with blood and held together by the sinews …

> a skeleton without flesh and blood, held together by the sinews …

> disconnected bones scattered in the main and intermediate directions, here a hand bone, elsewhere a foot bone, elsewhere a shin bone, elsewhere a thigh bone, elsewhere a hip bone, elsewhere a back bone, and elsewhere a skull …

a corpse thrown away in a charnel ground, bones bleached white, the colour of shells …

bones heaped up, more than a year old …

bones rotten and crumbling to dust, and one compares this same body with it: "This body too is of the same nature, it will be like that, it is not exempt from that fate."

The instructions speak of "comparing" our own body to the different stages of decay through which a corpse would go if it were left out in the open. Similar to the anatomical parts, the contemplation itself is not introduced as a form of mindfulness. Actually in the present case the exercise appears to involve some form of visualization. The text introduces the different stages of decay with the phrase "as though one were to see a corpse". The Pāli formulation leaves the door open for imagination and need not be concerned only with recollecting what we have actually seen.

The way these different stages of decay are presented gives the impression that we might just choose one of them, or alternatively proceed step by step through the entire series. The purpose of this contemplation appears to be twofold. One direction in which to take this practice becomes evident in the *Mahādukkhakkhandha-sutta* (MN 13; Anālayo 2003: 153f and 2013: 101f). The discourse contrasts the pleasure of seeing a beautiful and attractive young girl to her condition after she has passed away and her body is going through the stages of decay of a corpse, corresponding to those described in the *Satipaṭṭhāna-sutta*. This mode of understanding would make the present exercise similar in its basic orientation to contemplation of the anatomical parts.

RECOLLECTION OF DEATH

An alternative direction in which to take this practice, which is the approach that I will be presenting here, is to take this contemplation as a reflection on the mortality of the body. This to my mind is a topic of such importance that I definitely want to include it in the mode of practice I do myself and teach to others. If I were asked to recommend just one single meditation practice, I would probably opt for recollection of death. This is because of its transformative power.

In our modern society we have become so used to avoiding the fact of death. The different defence mechanisms employed to ignore our own mortality and that of others have been studied in detail in clinical psychology. A range of publications are available on what comes under the heading of Terror Management Theory (TMT). This is the *theory* that explains how human beings *manage* their existential *terror*.

Human beings share with animals the instinct for self-preservation. The case of human beings takes on a special turn because we are aware of the fact that death is unavoidable. The combination of the instinctive drive for self-preservation and the knowledge of the inevitability of death creates the potential for paralysing terror. As soon as death comes within the range of attention, human beings tend to react with various defence mechanisms. The most common ones are trying to distract oneself or else pushing the problem of death into the distant future.

As a consequence of being made aware of their mortality, human beings tend to cling strongly to their views and sense of identity as a way of fending off the feeling of being threatened. Just being briefly reminded of the fact of death makes individuals react in ways that are more narrow-minded and biased, as ways of fending off the realization of their own mortality.

The future Buddha's own search for liberation starts out with insight into his own mortality as one of the central dimensions of *dukkha* (together with disease and old age). A discourse in the *Aṅguttara-nikāya* reports his reflection that others, on seeing someone dead, tend to be repelled by it, ignoring the fact that they are themselves subject to the same fate (AN 3.38; Anālayo 2017c: 5ff). The Buddha-to-be realized the inappropriateness of this type of reaction. He allowed the truth that he was himself subject to the same fate sink into his mind. As a result, all his intoxication with being alive vanished.

According to the *Ariyapariyesanā-sutta* (MN 26; Anālayo 2013: 109f and 2017c: 8ff), together with manifestations of *dukkha* like old age and disease, the fact of death motivated the future Buddha to embark on his quest for awakening. Having successfully attained awakening, the Buddha proclaimed that he had realized the deathless. This is not some form of immortality. His body was still subject to passing away. But he was no longer affected by death, be it his own or that of others. In other words, according to early Buddhist thought, freedom from death can be realized while still alive.

It may well be that the realization of the future Buddha that he was subject to the same fate of death, which then led him to engage in the quest for what leads beyond death, is echoed in the formulation in the instruction given above. The *Satipaṭṭhāna-sutta* encourages the reflection that we are indeed "of the same nature" and we "will be like that" corpse in various stages of decay. In sum, we are "not exempt from that fate". These formulations could be employed for reflecting regularly on our own mortality and thereby building a foundation for applying this understanding during actual contemplation.

A PRACTICAL APPROACH

Actual practice can take as its starting point the image of a skeleton. This would be the "skeleton without flesh and blood, held together by the sinews" out of the different stages of decay described above. To begin with, we might simply bring to mind the image of a skeleton (or else another stage of decomposition we prefer). The mental image of the skeleton could be further strengthened if our whole-body awareness, to be practised throughout all the different exercises described in this book, were to be undertaken in such a way that prominence is given to the skeleton. This would build on the way of practice we did for the earlier two *satipaṭṭhāna* exercises, where with contemplation of the anatomical parts we explored the bones of the skeleton and with contemplation of the earth element we were to some extent still aware of the skeleton as part of our awareness of the solidity of the whole body. The main difference now is that, instead of becoming aware of the skeleton through a gradual sweep, we are simply aware of the whole skeleton inside our body, something with which we are by now familiar.

In this way, what has been introduced as an *object* with the help of a mental image of the skeleton of another now becomes the *subject* of contemplation by being directly related to the skeleton in our own living body. As a result, the fact of death becomes palpably *my* death. This can serve to actualize the reflection that "this body too is of the same nature, it will be like that, it is not exempt from that fate."

Needless to say, at the time of contemplation our own body is still alive, whereas a dead body is bereft of any felt sense of the stages of decomposition that it undergoes. Thus the exercise is about making a comparison, it is not about imagining how it feels when our own body falls apart. The purpose is only to drive home the fact that our own body will after death decompose, but that decomposition itself is not something that can any longer be felt.

For those who wish to undertake contemplation in a way that incorporates the entire description in the *Satipaṭṭhāna-sutta*, all of the different stages of decay could be brought into the practice. I would personally recommend getting started by working just with a single stage, such as the skeleton. Building on that, those who wish to do so could expand the practice to cover all of the different stages of decay described in the discourse. In what follows I briefly sketch one way in which this could be undertaken. For readers who are relatively new to facing mortality and the stages of decay, it might be preferable to skip over the next paragraph, as the description given in it can be somewhat unsettling.

Visualizing our own body as having just died, we might picture it gradually beginning to bloat and become livid, festering, and oozing matter. The digestive enzymes begin to eat up the stomach and the eyes bulge out. Crows come to pick out the eyes. The nostrils and the mouth are filled with maggots which start to eat the tongue and other fleshy parts. Maggots also eat their way into the brain. Hawks and vultures tear out the heart and the intestines, while dogs and jackals bite off the genitals and munch away at the limbs. Any remaining flesh on the body, after different animals have feasted on it, rots away. Eventually only the blood-smeared bones of the skeleton remain.

The sinews that kept the bones together as a skeleton decompose and the individual bones come to be scattered here and there. The scattered bones bleach, rot, and gradually crumble to dust.

The mode of practice suggested here clearly involves an element of visual imagination. As mentioned above, the formulation used in the actual instructions in the *Satipaṭṭhāna-sutta* speaks of comparing our body to what we would see in a charnel ground, which leaves open the door to an element of visual imagination.

A sense of the extent to which such visual imagination is successful and appropriate can be determined by noting whether it stings our sense of identity with, and ownership of, the body. The stage when animals eat various parts of our body can be particularly effective in this respect.

A related dimension can be cultivated when we are bitten by mosquitoes and ticks. Besides the actual itch, what additionally stings is often the unwelcome sense that our own body is food for others. By contemplating that this is its final destiny anyway, we can diminish and eventually completely overcome this additional sting.

Another interesting stage in the process of decomposition of the corpse comes when the skeleton disintegrates. As long as the skeleton is still held together by tendons, as long as it is still to some extent a compact unit, it looks like a person. Once the tendons have decomposed, however, the scattered bones no longer give rise to the perception of a person. This is similar to the sense conveyed by the butcher simile, mentioned in the last chapter, when the slaughtered cow turns into pieces of meat.

A related observation could be cultivated when hair and nails are being cut. Even though both are already dead matter while on the body, they are still perceived as an integral aspect of "our" body. This quickly changes once they are cut off and to be discarded.

The recommendation to notice whether it stings is of general relevance for *satipaṭṭhāna* meditation, and the present exercise is a particularly useful occasion for exploring the sting. In order to dwell independently and not cling to anything, it is helpful to identify our dependencies and what we cling to.

Whenever it stings, wherever there is agitation, it is right there that dependencies and clinging show up. It is right there that an opportunity manifests for gradually letting go of them.

THE BREATH AND IMPERMANENCE

In order to encourage further the facing of death with the present contemplation, I recommend that another exercise be combined with the vision of a decomposing corpse. This is recollection of death based on the breath. Although this is clearly not part of the *satipaṭṭhāna* scheme, such recollection is described in two discourses in the *Aṅguttara-nikāya* (AN 6.19 and AN 8.73; Anālayo 2016: 200ff).

The Buddha had been examining how some of his disciples were practising recollection of death. The different ways of practice they described were all based on pushing death away into the distance. Instead, the Buddha recommended that death should be brought directly into the present moment. We should be aware that we might die right after the present breath. As a practice related to eating, we could also be aware that we might die after having eaten the present morsel. The thrust of this recommendation is very much in line with the findings of Terror Management Theory. A chief defence mechanism against the threat of mortality is precisely to push death away into the distant future.

The contemplation of the corpse in decay can be substantially enhanced by being combined with the awareness that the present breath might be our last. Before going into the details of the practice, however, I need to mention that those with respiratory problems or those with suicidal tendencies should not adopt this practice. Moreover, a recommendation for anyone undertaking recollection of death is to do it very carefully and gradually. By way of illustration, imagine being given a very powerful car just after getting a driving licence. It would be rather foolish to drive that car at top speed on a busy highway. Similarly, with the present exercise it is important not to charge ahead too quickly.

Genuine wisdom is the result of gradual growth and cultivation, not of just trying to force our way through as quickly as possible.

A discourse in the *Aṅguttara-nikāya* compares the threefold training in morality, concentration, and wisdom to a farmer who plants his crop and waters it in due time (AN 3.91; Anālayo 2003: 253). That much is what the farmer can do, but he is not able to force the crop to become ripe right on the spot. The same patient attitude of planting the seeds of wisdom and growing the seeds of insight by watering them in due time through meditation practice is appropriate for the present exercise (as well as for *satipaṭṭhāna* in general). We do the needful and allow what we have planted to ripen gradually and eventually bear its liberating fruits. In contrast, to attempt to force our way through can easily become an assertion of the ego and thereby run counter to the balance appropriate for genuine growth of insight. Such a forceful attitude would also conflict with insight into not-self, cultivated with the previous contemplation of the elements.

Becoming aware of the breath takes up a manifestation of the wind element that has already come to our attention with the final stage in the contemplation of the elements. The element on which the body urgently depends for its survival is precisely the wind element (in the form of oxygen supply), the most ephemeral of the four elements. In this way, contemplation of the elements has already alerted us to the precariousness of bodily existence.

We continue with the same theme by combining awareness of the constant flow of oxygen in and out with the recognition that the body's survival depends entirely on the uninterrupted continuity of this supply of oxygen. The breath is what connects us to life. With this form of practice, we are *connecting* with that which *connects* us to life. This connection is nothing but a flow, an arising of a changing flow of air and its passing away. It is so utterly impermanent and insubstantial. Our body depends entirely on this constantly changing process of breathing. How could such a body be permanent? This is impossible.

The present exercise is particularly apt for exploring the nature of arising and passing away in relation to the body. This is the second aspect mentioned in the refrain, which builds on the internal and external dimensions of practice mentioned before in the refrain. These have already been explored with the anatomical parts and the elements. Actually the internal and external dimensions are so self-evident when we contemplate the elements that they can hardly be missed. The same holds for impermanence in relation to the present exercise. It is so self-evident that it can hardly be missed.

Needless to say, impermanence is also relevant to contemplation of the anatomical parts and the elements, just as the internal and external dimensions of practice apply also to the present exercise. In fact the death of others can for some practitioners become a natural entry door into recollection of death. When following this mode of approach, however, it would still be worth ensuring that this does not become a way of avoiding the facing of our own death.

The present practice involves giving full attention to the cutting edge of impermanence, to the fact that impermanence means that this very body will sooner or later pass away. It is for this reason that this exercise can become a particularly powerful mode of implementing the instruction in the refrain to contemplate the nature of arising and of passing away. The continuity of the body, which so easily is just taken for granted, entirely depends on the constant arising and passing away of the breath. And the breath itself is so palpably impermanent, it is nothing but a changing flow.

This dependency on the breath at the same time exemplifies the empty nature of the body, which had already become apparent with the contemplation of the elements. We are of course to some extent in control over the body; we do take decisions when moving its limbs or positioning it in this way or that way. There is naturally a sense of a temporary degree of ownership and identity. We are able to distinguish between our own body and that of another. But such control and ownership are limited; they operate within a network of conditions of which several are outside the range of our full control and ownership.

We are not in sole and complete control over the body, otherwise the body would just be the way we want it. It would never get sick and certainly not pass away. We are also not the sole and true owners of this body. As mentioned in the previous chapter, elements taken in from the outside in the form of food and drink at some point during this process are experienced as having become "mine". Yet soon enough some of this intake turns into faeces and urine to be discarded, and whatever remains in the body will definitely leave the sphere of our sense of ownership with death. In this way, death serves to clarify the implications of the impermanent and empty nature of the body.

There will come a time when the breath stops flowing and this body will die. If it were left out in the open, it would go through the stages of decay of a corpse described in the *Satipaṭṭhāna-sutta*. Having recollected whatever visual image of a corpse we have decided to adopt, with each breath we can become aware that this might be our last breath. The perception arises that we could die even right now, as a result of which the gradual decay of our own body would start very soon. We cannot be sure that our breathing continues beyond what is happening in the present moment. Once this uncertainty is appreciated, we no longer take breathing for granted.

For actual practice I recommend relating this type of awareness in particular to the inhalation. With every exhalation we can in turn cultivate an attitude of relaxing and letting go, training ourselves in the best way of facing the moment of dying. With these two modes it becomes possible to fine-tune the practice to our personal needs. Adjustments can take place by giving more attention either to the inhalations or to the exhalations. This does not mean changing the nature or length of the breath in any way. Breathing remains natural breathing. The point is solely about where to direct mental attention.

At times the fact of our own mortality does not really sink into the mind. When mindfully noticing this, we can give more emphasis to the inhalations and the fact that this could be our last breath. At other times the mind can get agitated. As we become aware of this, we give more emphasis to the exhalations, to letting go and relaxing. In this way it becomes possible to adjust the practice in such a way that progress can be achieved while at the same time maintaining balance of the mind.

Facing our own mortality through the practice of what I like to call "death-breath", relating the certainty of our own death to the experience of the breath, is facing ignorance head-on.

There is hardly anything else that human beings would like to ignore as much as the fact of their own death. This explains the defence mechanisms identified by research related to Terror Management Theory. It is therefore not at all surprising if this type of meditation practice provokes reactions. It would be unreasonable to expect that things just go smoothly.

The challenging nature of the present practice receives some cushioning through the preparatory work done with the two previous body contemplations. The cultivation of non-attachment through contemplation of the anatomical parts facilitates a lessening of identification with the body, whose empty nature is revealed through contemplation of the elements. Both exercises together engender an attitude towards the body that is less dominated by clinging and a sense of ownership. This in turn prepares the ground for being able to face squarely the fact that this body will eventually fall apart; it is certainly not exempt from that fate.

Still, the practice will quite probably lead to reactions. A common type of reaction is mental cloudiness and lack of clarity. This is when ignorance manifests its deluding force. At such times, the fact of mortality just fails to impact the mind. The mental reflection seems just hollow phrases and the exercise appears to be meaningless. It is helpful to note that this is just what we would expect. The forces of ignorance have for a long time been in control of the mind. They can hardly be expected to yield right away and just disappear. Instead, it takes the sustained effort of a gradual approach to diminish and eventually emerge from this type of ignorance.

One helpful tool in this respect is giving importance to being in the present moment. This counteracts the tendency of ignorance to turn the practice into something done automatically or by rote. Opening up to the changing nature of present-moment experience helps us to get out of the autopilot mode. Once that has been achieved, awareness of the fragility of this present moment can be introduced by way of recalling our dependence on the breath.

The reflection that the next breath might be the last can be further strengthened by adding another reflection: "Even if this breath is not the last, it is certainly one breath closer to death." We do not know when death will happen but we do know that it certainly will happen. With every breath we are definitely coming closer to the time of our death. The breath right now is one "breath less" until eventually we will be completely "breathless".

There is nothing surprising in this: mortality is the birthday present every human body receives right at the time of coming into existence. Nevertheless, it takes much courage and effort to face what most human beings run away from: death is certain.

Another tool, to be used carefully and judiciously, is to hold the breath. We breathe out and do not breathe in again for a little while. Briefly holding the breath in this way, we soon notice the urge to breathe in again. This helps to bring home to us the precariousness of our physical existence and the uncertainty of being able to take the next breath.

Holding the breath should not become a continuous form of practice. In other words, the present suggestion is not meant to encourage some form of breath retention. Doing so would risk losing sight of a chief characteristic of mindfulness practice in general, which is uninvolved observation. In relation to the breath this means that the task is to observe the breath as it is, rather than influencing it in any way. To hold the breath once is more like an alarm clock, whose purpose is to wake us up. It would not make sense for the alarm clock to keep ringing all the time. It has fulfilled its function once we wake up. Similarly, when holding the breath once has woken us up to the precariousness of our existence, we continue cultivating awareness of that precariousness with normal breathing as it naturally occurs, without interfering with it.

The opposite type of reaction under the influence of ignorance is fear and agitation: "This is too much, I am not able to handle this!" Whenever that happens, we immediately give emphasis to letting go and relaxing. By calming the mind and reassuring ourselves that we are able to face the truth of our own mortality, the tendency to become agitated can be gradually overcome.

FACING MORTALITY

The *Dhātuvibhaṅga-sutta* refers to the type of feeling experienced by an accomplished practitioner close to death as a category of its own, encouraging its contemplation in the same way as the three types of feeling taken up under the second *satipaṭṭhāna* (to be discussed in the next chapter). The pattern is invariably that, when feeling a certain type of feeling, one knows: "I feel this type of feeling." Here this pattern is applied to feeling qualified as "ending with life" (*jīvitapariyantika*; MN 140).

Those who have been really close to death know the distinct affective tone of being on the brink of passing away, the intensity and resultant total presence of the mind, which at times comes with a different sense of time, as if everything were in slow motion. With sustained practice of recollection of death in the way described above, this intensity and total presence can at times come to accompany our meditative facing of our own mortality. A distinct difference, however, is that painful feelings of distress and dread are being replaced by neutral feelings of mental equipoise.

Becoming in this way accomplished in facing death makes a substantial contribution not only to the actual moment of dying, but also to daily life. Having learned to face death with equipoise nourishes an inner peace that remains unshaken by the vicissitudes of life. All it takes to gain this vantage point of inner imperturbability is a sustained effort in the meditative practice of facing our own mortality.

At some uncertain point in the future we will have to face death anyway. This is certain. Who knows what the conditions will be at that time? We might be sick and in pain, surrounded by others who are crying and upset, with unfinished things looming in the air and worries burdening our mind. If we do not prepare ourselves, it will be very difficult to face death in such a situation.

The time to prepare for death is right here and now. When else could it be? Just as we would not start to study only on the day of examination, just as we would not start to train only on the day of competition, similarly it is not a good idea to wait for the time of dying in order to prepare for death. Such preparations are better done in advance, when we are reasonably healthy and able to approach the fact of our mortality gradually. Learning to face our mortality step by step, we are training in the art of dying. Training in the art of dying is at the same time training in the art of living.

Recollection of death is not only a preparation for dying, but also a way of coming fully alive. Being aware of our own mortality and that of others makes it unmistakeably clear that the present moment is the only time when we can live. By facing our own shadow of death, instead of running away from it, we gradually become whole. This is actually a process of healing, by allowing death to become an integral part of our life. Death is inseparable from life; ignoring its existence, we can never live fully.

Awareness of our mortality also encourages us to be completely with those we meet. Who knows: I might die or the person I meet might die. Therefore, let me make best use of the present moment by giving my full attention to whoever I meet. Let me be with them to the utmost of my ability such that, if death should separate us, there will be no regrets. There will be nothing left unsaid that I would rather have communicated, nothing left unsolved that I would rather have clarified, and, most important of all, nothing left to forgive that I would rather have forgiven or apologized for.

Recollection of death clarifies our priorities in life. In the face of our mortality, how should we live our lives in such a way that we can die without regrets? As a supportive exercise for such reflection, I recommend taking death out for a solitary walk. During such a walk, we might reflect on what would happen if we were not to come back from this walk. What would happen to our possessions, friends, and relatives, our role and function in society?

Reflecting in this way, we increasingly learn to let go of clinging to possessions, with the understanding that anyway we cannot keep them forever. We readily forgive those who have wronged us and become willing to apologize quickly whenever we have hurt others. We learn to let go of the tendency to try to manipulate or force others to be or act the way we want.

If I were to die now, they would do things their own way in any case. So let me give them my support and guidance in an open manner, without trying to force them to do things my way and without creating dependencies. Reflecting in this way lessens our attachment to our role, job, and function within our social network. We do our best, without depending too much on the results and with the clear understanding that sooner or later others will continue without us. Our priorities become clarified. What is it that I really want to do before I move on? What really matters to me?

The transformative power of recollection of death makes it indeed worthwhile to dedicate time to its practice and cultivation, be this in formal sitting, during daily activities, or by way of reflection. Recollection of our mortality can be supported by repeated reminders during everyday life. Seeing road kill or passing by a cemetery can serve as such direct reminders of death. In addition, we are surrounded by so many things that have been designed and manufactured by others who in the meantime have passed away. Once we are willing to attend to death, a broad range of possible reminders offer themselves. Every single act of such recollection is another step to counter ignorance, the ingrained tendency to ignore our own death. Every such step makes its contribution to bringing us gradually closer to the realization of the deathless.

In addition, giving attention only to the skeleton can be continued during various activities. Shifting from sitting to walking meditation, we just remain aware of the skeleton. Walking as a skeleton, standing as a skeleton, eating as a skeleton, lying down to rest as a skeleton; there is no limit to the activities that can be carried out with awareness of our own skeleton. Practising in this way keeps alive the fact of our mortality.

Awareness of the skeleton can in fact be used as a convenient summary of all three body contemplations. With the skeleton all sexually attractive parts are gone and we would not have any sensual desire for it. Similarly, all markers of identity are gone. It is hardly possible for us to recognize the identity of a particular skeleton, leaving little room for considering it to be "me" or "mine". Combined with using the skeleton as a reminder of mortality, this single mode of attention can activate central themes of all three body contemplations.

THE ELEMENTS AND DEATH

Yet another mode of practice relates recollection of death to the elements. This can be undertaken by visualizing the stages of dying. At first, when death comes close, the body feels heavy and control over the limbs of the body is gradually lost. The dying might try to remove their blanket (if they are still able to do so) to alleviate the general feeling of being oppressed by some weight. This is the stage when the earth element begins to disintegrate. Those who care for the dying might notice their increasing inability to move. Moreover, on trying to lift up the dying they might find them to be subjectively heavier. This is because with the disintegration of the earth element the structure of the body loses its solidity. Therefore it becomes more difficult to lift up and move around a person who has reached this stage of dying.

With the next stage the dying person loses control over the bodily liquids. This is the beginning of the disintegration of the water element. The mouth dries up and the person becomes thirsty. Outside observers can notice water coming out of the eyes and drops of urine out of the urethra. At times the dying might open their mouth and stretch out their tongue as if wanting to drink.

With the next stage the fire element begins to dissolve. The body starts to lose its temperature. A sense of coldness moves from the tips of the toes and the fingers gradually towards the heart. Those who are by the side of the dying person might notice that feet and hands turn bluish and at times the person starts to shiver. Whereas at the time of the dissolution of the earth element the dying might try to remove their blanket, at this stage they prefer to be covered in order to prevent the loss of heat.

The final stage comes with the dissolution of the wind element. The dying person experiences great difficulty in taking in the required amount of oxygen. The inhalations are visibly shorter and strained, the exhalations longer and weaker. The whole process of breathing becomes more and more laboured until with a last exhalation it ceases completely.

Visualizing ourselves going through these stages of dying can become a powerful way of cultivating recollection of death. At the same time, it offers a useful preparation for the time of dying. Of course, we might die suddenly in an accident. But chances are that the events leading up to our death will involve these stages. Familiarizing ourselves with them through meditative practice and recollection helps to recognize what is happening and face it with a balanced mind. It also helps to recognize what others might be going through at the time of dying and enables us to know how they can best be assisted.

OPEN PRACTICE

Contemplation of the anatomical parts has imbued our practice with a sense of non-attachment, and contemplation of the elements has instilled in our practice a taste of freedom from identification. Building on these, contemplation of death establishes a powerful perception of impermanence through recognition of our own mortality. Based on the foundation laid by these three body contemplations, we move on to an unstructured mode of practice by opening up the vista of our awareness to anything that happens in the present moment. Proceeding in this way, we are gradually coming closer to the experience of the deathless.

Whereas contemplation of the anatomical parts and elements has rooted mindfulness in the body, contemplation of death firmly establishes us in the present moment, the only time when we can truly live. This is the contribution made by contemplation of death to the hub of the wheel of practice: coming fully alive to the present moment. The contribution made to the rim of the wheel is a substantial diminishing of clinging and attachment through the realization that we would have to let go anyway when we die. We learn to face the terror of our own mortality, the cutting edge of impermanence. This substantially nourishes our ability to dwell independently without clinging to anything.

SUMMARY

Contemplation of a corpse in decay can be employed to reveal the body's lack of inherent beauty or else its mortality. By way of implementing the second alternative, we can combine the mental image of a skeleton (or of another stage of decay) with awareness of respiration, keeping in mind the uncertainty of being able to take even the next breath.

Such contemplation is best undertaken with a keen eye on balance. Here giving attention either to the inhalations or to the exhalations can be employed to maintain balance. Attention to inhalations can be yoked to recollection of our mortality in order to strengthen the practice, while attention to exhalations can come with an attitude of relaxing and letting go in order to calm the mind if it becomes too agitated.

Undertaken in a balanced but sustained manner, such practice helps to drive home the undeniable fact that death is certain, and that it could in principle happen even right now. Learning in this way to allow death to become part of our life, our priorities become clarified and we learn to live more fully in the present.

VI

FEELING

The fourth spoke in the wheel of practice presented here and at the same time the second *satipaṭṭhāna* is contemplation of feeling. The Pāli term for feeling is *vedanā*, which stands for the affective tone or the hedonic quality of experience, its tonality. The term *vedanā* does not refer to emotions. Emotions are a more complex phenomenon and would find a better placing under the rubric of mental states, which is the topic of the next *satipaṭṭhāna*.

The first part of the instruction for contemplation of feelings proceeds as follows (MN 10):

> When feeling a pleasant feeling, one knows: "I feel a pleasant feeling"; when feeling a painful feeling, one knows: "I feel a painful feeling"; when feeling a neutral feeling, one knows: "I feel a neutral feeling."

The three types of feeling mentioned in the instruction are best viewed as part of a continuous bandwidth of what is affectively known, a spectrum that ranges from the most pleasurable to the most painful of feeling tones. Somewhere in the medium part of this range of felt experiences there is an area which is literally "not-painful-not-pleasant" (*adukkhamasukha*). Each practitioner needs to stake out the precise compass of this area through mindful observation. Ongoing practice of contemplation of feeling will make it clear what types of feeling tone are best reckoned as being neither painful enough to be able to lead to any aversion nor pleasant enough to trigger any desire. It is these types that can be considered "neutral", and the range of felt experience to either side of them can go under the labels of "pleasant" and "painful" (or at least "unpleasant") feeling.

Attention given to neutral feelings helps to avoid a dualistic distinction between painful and pleasant feelings as if these were two totally distinct phenomena. Instead, pleasure and pain are dimensions of a continuum of felt experience, with a middle section that is neither distinctly pleasant nor really painful.

FEELING AND REACTIVITY

The chief task with contemplation of feeling is to ask ourselves the question: "How do you feel?" This question needs to be asked with a sincere and genuine interest of really wanting to know. The reason why this enquiry carries such significance is that usually the affective input of feeling directly leads to a reaction.

When experiencing pleasant feelings, the tendency is to react with desire and clinging, wanting to keep the pleasure and have more of it. With painful feelings, the tendency of the mind is to react with aversion and irritation, wanting it to stop and disappear, never to occur again. In the case of neutral feelings, the mind tends to get bored and search for some more entertaining distraction. Neutral feelings do not hold the promise of something new and exciting, hence they easily stimulate the tendency to ignorance, to quite literally being ignored.

Contemplation of feeling shines the light of awareness on these ingrained tendencies. It replaces the ignorance of automatic reaction with the knowledge of clear recognition. We train ourselves not to ignore the impact of the affective dimension of experience. This can offer substantial help in everyday situations. Having learned to be aware of the affective dimension of experience makes it easier to detect what is happening in the mind at an early stage. Such mental happenings usually start on the affective level, when a particular feeling leads to subsequent unskilful reactions and proliferations. Once mindfulness is established on the level of feeling, it becomes possible to recognize an unwholesome reaction before it has acquired full force. Recognition at such an early stage makes it possible to nip this reaction in the bud.

Moreover, if mindfulness has not been swift enough to catch things at an early stage, even at any later moment in the trajectory of the building up of mental negativity the spotlight on feeling helps bring us back to an element of simplicity in the present moment. The affective push of feeling operates during any stage of mental elaboration. Its mindful recognition offers a door into disentangling complexity. Based on this type of grounding, it becomes easier to cultivate an appropriate response to whatever is happening, on the internal and on the external level.

This remarkable potential would explain why feelings have been selected as the topic of a whole *satipaṭṭhāna*, in between the body and mental states. The present exercise in fact directs attention to a crucial link in dependent arising (*paṭicca samuppāda*). Feeling is the place where craving can arise. In a way, feeling is what makes the world go round. But it does not have to be that way. Although craving can manifest in response to feeling, it does not have to manifest. Through mindful recognition it becomes possible to avoid the arising of craving.

The speed with which feelings usually lead to a reaction can be appreciated by imagining an earlier stage in the evolution of the human species. Picture a Neanderthal turning a corner in a jungle and suddenly seeing something ahead. Within a split second a decision has to be taken. Is this something I can eat or is this something that can eat me? The speed of the decision between fight and flight is crucial for survival. Feeling offers an important input for making such quick decisions. In the average modern-day living situation, however, the speed of such reactivity triggered by feeling can have detrimental consequences. It can lead us into ways of acting and reacting that we would not have chosen if we had allowed sufficient time for sober reflection. Turning the light of awareness on feelings, we can learn to pause with mindfulness and become aware of their impact before being carried away by our reactions.

A PRACTICAL APPROACH

In actual practice I suggest using the body scan again. During the earlier scans, the task was to be aware of the anatomical parts or the elements in the body. This was based on combining the map of our knowledge of the constitution of the body with feeling the body. With the present exercise this same feeling of the body during the scan can be used to turn attention more inwards towards feeling itself.

An example to illustrate such turning more inwards would be if we shift our attention for a moment to the experience of holding this book in our hands. Touching the paper of the book we can know the material out of which it is made. In this case, attention is directed towards the object held in the hands. The very same experience can also be taken in the other direction by being aware of the act of touching. In this case, attention is instead directed towards the hands. Similarly, with contemplation of feeling the same type of scan is used to explore that which feels the body.

To get started, at first we might do scans for individual feelings. With a first scan from head to feet we could explore in particular the occurrence of any pleasant feeling somewhere on the surface or in the interior of the body. During a second scan from feet to head we could see if any painful feeling manifests anywhere in or on the body. A third scan from head to feet could be to discover any neutral feelings in or on the body. Based on growing familiarity with the three types of feeling, we might at times find it more convenient to combine all three into a single mode of attending to feelings. Whatever feelings we encounter during a scan, be these feelings of smoothness or roughness, throbbing or pulsing, pressure or lightness, tension or ease, or any other type, there is no need to get involved with the details of their individual manifestations. We only give importance to their hedonic tone, their affective quality. In short, we just recognize whether they are experienced as pleasant, unpleasant, or neutral.

After having done such scanning, we remain aware of the whole body in the sitting posture and of the manifestation of any feeling of these three types. With the occurrence of any feeling, we just keep noticing its affective tone.

Having explored the manifestation of feelings in and on the body, we continue by opening up the vista of our awareness to noticing any type of feelings, even those that do not have a prominent impact on the somatic level. Hearing a sound, for example, we might note the affective tone that accompanies our recognition and mental processing of that sound. The same goes for the other senses. In this way, we learn to be continuously aware of the affective dimension of our experience. Moreover, we come to distinguish more clearly if a particular feeling started on the bodily level or because of mental evaluation.

Contemplation of feelings can become a powerful tool for shining the light of awareness on mental events. This potential lies in the relative simplicity of the affective tone of feelings, compared to the comparatively more complex character of other aspects of mental activity. Trying to remain aware while the mind is engaged in some thought activity is more easily said than done, as thought easily draws us in and soon enough we find ourselves immersed in the thinking rather than watching it. Yet *satipaṭṭhāna* meditation is not something to be carried out only in the absence of thought. On the contrary, it needs to encompass all possible situations, be this in formal practice or when moving out into the world. Unless we learn in some way to remain mindful while the mind is active, how will we ever be able to carry our mindfulness practice along into daily life? Therefore finding a way of learning to be mindful when the mind is engaged in thought is an important requirement.

Here feelings offer a convenient training ground. Due to their simplicity, feelings are somewhat like a handle that we can use to take hold of the complexity of mental events without getting caught up in them. In this way, when the mind is involved in thinking, perhaps even in emotional reactions, this need not be considered an obstruction to practice. Instead, it can become an opportunity to train ourselves in a skill of considerable importance. This is the ability to remain aware of the basic affective tone of present-moment experience. Such tuning in on the affective level provides a grounding; it can serve as an anchor that prevents our being carried away by what is taking place.

Of the three types of feeling, the neutral type is the one usually ignored. When faced with this sort of unexciting experience, the tendency of the untrained mind is to shift quickly to something else, to go out in search of some sort of distraction. The inability to just be with neutral feelings can be responsible for a tendency to dramatize whatever happens and coat experience with an overlay of likes and dislikes. Anything can serve as a building block to intensify the affective tonality of what is happening to us, be it on the pleasant or the unpleasant side, as long as it triggers the excitement of strong feelings and takes us out of the blandness of neutral ones. The inevitable results of giving free rein to this tendency are biased perceptions and unbalanced reactions, in short: ignorance is in full swing. As a way of countering this potential of neutral feelings to activate the drama of ignorance, we can make a conscious effort to remain aware of neutral feelings, no longer ignoring them.

At times, however, it can also happen that we are not able to feel any feeling, even neutral ones. In such a case we simply note that. Similar to the earlier body scans, where it was not necessary to experience distinctly each anatomical part or element in every part of the body, in the present case the successful carrying out of the contemplation also does not depend on being able to distinctly sense feelings in every part of the body. The purpose of the practice is to understand the way feelings impact the mind. To serve this purpose, it is sufficient to experience some feelings of the different types. It is not necessary to overcome first of all any blank area in the body so as to have a totally comprehensive experience of feelings.

THE PUSH OF FEELINGS

The impact of feelings on the mind can be explored in particular when we encounter unpleasant or painful feelings. Some of these could be due to chronic pain. In such cases we simply note the feeling and move on with our scan. If such pain becomes strong, we create space around it by being aware of the whole body rather than focusing on the pain alone. It can sometimes be useful to note if there are other parts of the body that are not in pain. This helps to remain balanced.

Other unpleasant or painful feelings encountered during the scan could be simply due to the sitting posture, or else some itch may have arisen. In such cases, the practice can be more focused on the pain. The recommendation is to stay with the painful feeling for a little while, observing the unpleasant sensation or the itch together with the push that manifests in the mind. The object of observation is the push of feeling, clamouring for our attention and for a reaction to take place, for some action to be undertaken to stop the itch or unpleasant feeling.

The task here is not to sit through excruciating pain. We are not trying to turn *satipaṭṭhāna* into an ascetic practice. The task is only to stay for a short while and observe unpleasant feelings in their conditionality. We observe unpleasant feelings in order to understand how these affect the mind. This offers an opportunity for developing our own personal and direct experience of dependent arising. All it takes is noticing that push.

After the push has been noticed, we are free to take action. We scratch or change our posture, according to what the situation demands. We notice the pleasant feelings of relief and the mental reaction of wanting this pleasure to last. Needless to say, pleasant feelings can push the mind just as much as unpleasant feelings. The recommendation is only to begin exploring the push of feelings with the case of pain, as this offers an easily accessible and evident occasion for such exploration. Once understood, the push can be noticed with any type of feelings, at times perhaps even by noticing the subtle push of neutral feelings for something more entertaining.

With sustained practice of noting this push, eventually the experience of each of the three types of feeling comes with an inbuilt awareness of their corresponding tendency. Pleasant feeling tends to attract, unpleasant feeling tends to rouse resistance, and neutral feeling tends to trigger the search for something else that is less boring. Our appreciation of the relationship of feelings to the underlying tendencies deepens. This in turn makes us realize the remarkable degree to which our apparently so well-reasoned evaluations and reactions are in truth and fact influenced by the affective tone of the type of feeling experienced.

Increasing familiarity with internal manifestations of the push exerted by feelings naturally leads over to noting the same also externally, when it manifests in others. Such noting reveals the extent to which other human beings are also under the sway of feelings in their apperceptions and subsequent actions. Being able to notice such an influence can be of considerable aid in communications and interactions with others.

Returning to formal meditation practice, subsequent to scanning the body we move on to being aware of any feelings that manifest, independent of whether their arising has a noticeable impact on the body or not. Some feelings hardly affect the body at all, wherefore their mindful observation needs to take place within the realm of the mind. Whatever type of feeling manifests, the task is throughout to be aware of the affective dimension of present-moment experience. Whenever this affective experience comes with a particularly prominent push, we try to notice it.

The advantage of cultivating awareness of feelings lies in coming to know and recognize what acts as an intermediary between body and mind. Feelings could be visualized as a messenger between what happens in the body and what takes place in the mind. Or else feelings can be considered an interface between body and mind. Through the medium of feelings, mental states can affect the condition of the body, just as, through the same medium of feelings, the condition of the body has its impact on the mind (Anālayo 2013: 121f). This perhaps explains why a discourse in the *Satipaṭṭhāna-saṃyutta* stipulates the cultivation of all four *satipaṭṭhānas* for a penetrative understanding (*pariññā*) of the three types of feeling (SN 47.49). Even though these three types are taken up in detail just with contemplation of feeling, apparently the cooperative effort made with the help of cultivating the other three *satipaṭṭhānas* puts the exploration done with the second *satipaṭṭhāna* into its proper context. This ensures that the resulting insight indeed becomes penetrative.

Feelings are conditioned and conditioning at the same time. They are conditioned by the type of contact that has led to their arising. This could be contact by way of bodily touch. But it could also be contact through another physical sense-door or through the mind-door on its own, such as when having a particular thought or idea.

The variety of feelings comes not only from the type of contact that leads to their arising. Their actual manifestations also differ. Feelings tend to affect both body and mind. But they do so to differing degrees. The felt experience of a mental state like anger has a stronger bodily component (physical tenseness, facial expression, etc.) than the feelings that arise with other mental states such as, for example, conceit.

In view of this variety, it is important to cultivate contemplation of feelings in a comprehensive manner. Contemplating only feelings that manifest as physical sensations would risk missing out on feelings that come with mental states that do not have a prominent relation to easily discerned bodily sensations. Such restricting of contemplation to only those feelings that manifest as bodily sensation would significantly narrow the scope of the present exercise and thereby miss out on a substantial portion of its liberating potential.

THE BODY AND PAIN

Nevertheless, bodily sensations are a prominent area for this contemplation. Sustained practice of the body scan with attention given to feelings reveals the surprising degree to which the body is a constant source of pain. Sitting in meditation, sooner or later bodily pain forces us to change posture. Even the posture of lying down cannot be maintained for long periods without eventually giving rise to pain and the need to turn around and change the body's position.

Aside from the pain inherent in the body when motionless in any posture, there is the irritation caused by the outside temperature. Now it is too hot, soon enough it is too cold. A constant need keeps forcing us to adjust clothing or turn on a fan or the heating in order to prevent this body from giving rise to pain due to temperature.

Another dimension of the same predicament is the need for food and drink. So much attention, time, and resources are spent catering to what we would like to eat and what we would like to drink. Gratifying our likes, as well as creating and enforcing such likes in others, receives a great deal of attention and publicity. But the truth of the matter is that we have to eat and we have to drink, simply to avoid the pain of hunger and thirst. When that pain has successfully been addressed at least for a short while, the inevitable result is the need to defecate and urinate. Failing to do these will become yet another source of pain. From the restaurant to the restroom, all these are just facilities for pain relief.

Taking a deep breath feels so pleasant. Why is that? Because for a moment the constant demand of the body for oxygen has been satisfied. We have to breathe in order to avoid the pain of lack of oxygen.

Contemplating the different dimensions of bodily pain can also be related to the elements, the second spoke in the wheel of practice presented here. The basic pain of the body in any posture due to the pressure of the body's weight, along with the need to eat and defecate, is a form of bodily pain that reflects the impact of the earth element. The need to drink and urinate relate to the water element. The necessity to maintain the body at a certain temperature points to the fire element. Out of various bodily motions, the need to breathe is a particularly prominent example of the potential for pain related to the wind element.

Aside from its place within contemplation of feelings, the constant subtle pain inherent in having a body can become an exercise on its own. All it takes is to note the amount of time and activity spent throughout the day just for the sake of maintaining the body in a less than painful condition: sleeping, eating, drinking, dressing, washing, and so on.

This type of contemplation or reflection can lead to a notable transformation of our attitude towards the body. It not only has a rather sobering effect on the pursuit of bodily pleasures in their various forms, it also can be of remarkable help in the case of illness. Bodily sensuality and bodily sickness are in fact two sides of the same coin. To whatever degree we become attached to the body through the pursuit of sensual pleasure, to that same degree we will suffer when the body is sick and in pain.

Another aspect of the same practice is that often the experience of the pain of disease comes with an implicit assumption that we are in some way entitled to health. Somehow it seems almost unfair that we should get sick and experience pain. Proper assessment of the true nature of the body as something that naturally gives rise to pain will help to free us of this unreasonable assumption. It is natural for the body to give rise to pain. There is nothing unfair or even surprising in this. Such understanding makes it easier to face any bodily pain with mental composure.

The physical experience of pain usually comes in combination with the mental pain of anguish and worry, caused by the bodily pain. The *Salla-sutta* illustrates this situation with the example of being shot by arrows (SN 36.6; Anālayo 2013: 120f and 2016: 27ff). When we experience physical pain without giving rise to mental affliction, we are similar to someone who is hit by one arrow only. Reacting with anguish and worry, however, is like being shot at by an additional arrow. With mindfulness present, this additional and unnecessary arrow can be avoided. The feelings experienced will quite literally be "ending with the body" (*kāyapariyantika*), rather than leading on to additional feelings caused by mental reactivity.

This can become a direct experiential approach to right view in terms of the four noble truths. Being mentally afflicted by the experience of pain is an obvious manifestation of the first truth of *dukkha*. The second arrow of mental anguish and worry arises due to craving for being without pain, exemplifying the teaching of the second truth on the role of craving. The situation of experiencing only the first arrow without any mental reactivity points to the third truth regarding (at least momentary) freedom from the *dukkha* of anguish and worry. The practice of mindfulness of feeling can serve as the practical path to achieving increasing degrees of freedom from such anguish and worry in relation to the physical experience of pain.

The early discourses clearly recognize that mindfulness offers a powerful tool with which to face the painful feelings of a disease. A discourse in the *Saṃyutta-nikāya* reports that Anuruddha, an eminent disciple gifted with exceptional concentrative abilities, faced the pain of serious sickness just with mindfulness (SN 52.10; Anālayo 2013: 135 and 2016: 53). Another discourse reports the Buddha himself employing mindfulness when sick (SN 1.38; Anālayo 2016: 61). Both cases are remarkable because the Buddha and Anuruddha could instead have used their concentrative powers to suppress the experience of pain. Instead of just switching off, they both opted to face pain with mindfulness. I take this to point to the power that inheres in contemplation of feelings, in particular when these are of the painful type.

THE MIND AND JOY

In addition to noticing the subtle pain inherent in having a body, sustained practice of the present contemplation will also reveal another feeling. Fortunately this is a pleasant one. It is the very subtle joy of being in the present moment. Noticing this subtle joy counterbalances the discovery of the pain inherent in having a body. Both types of feelings are ordinarily not noticed. It takes time and practice to recognize them.

The subtle pleasant feelings of being in the present moment are easily missed because of the mind's tendency to distraction. Another cause for being unable to notice this particular pleasant feeling can be if we become too pushy and overly exert ourselves. The resultant tension in the mind prevents the subtle joy of being in the present moment from arising. In this way, being able to note this subtle joy offers direct feedback on whether we have reached a balance point between becoming too loose, resulting in distraction, and too tight, resulting in contraction. Just as a lute whose strings are neither too tense nor too loose will produce melodious sound (AN 6.55; Anālayo 2003: 38), so the mind that is in a comparable condition of balance will produce the melodious sound of subtle joy.

Once this type of pleasant feeling has been recognized, it is in principle accessible in any situation. Even the most boring chore can become an occasion for experiencing subtle joy, as long as the chore is carried out with awareness well established in the present moment. The same holds for waiting at the dentist, being caught in a traffic jam, standing in a queue; there is no end to the opportunities for coming back to the present moment and turning what could easily be experienced as unpleasant into an occasion for the arising of wholesome pleasant feelings.

Consciously cultivating the presence of this subtle type of pleasant feeling can go a long way in countering the mind's inherent tendency to distraction. After all, the most prominent reason for distractions to occur is the mind's search for something more entertaining and pleasurable. By yoking our meditation practice to the experience of this refined joy of being in the present moment, the mind naturally tends to stay with the practice in the here and now, rather than moving off in search of something else. Therefore, I would recommend making recognition of the subtle pleasant feeling that arises from being in the present moment as much as possible a baseline for practice of the second *satipaṭṭhāna*. Once arisen, this refined type of feeling can be contemplated fairly continuously (as long as we remain mindful of the present moment, of course). In this way contemplation of feeling, besides its other manifold benefits, also yields an immediate payoff in relation to the main task of *satipaṭṭhāna* meditation: helping us to remain with awareness in the here and now. Being established on this baseline observational vantage point in the present moment makes it easy to notice when at times other (and usually stronger) types of feeling arise, which can then become the object of the mind in a comprehensive practice of the second *satipaṭṭhāna*.

A central realization that emerges from undertaking contemplation of feeling as described above is the insight into the affective potential of body and mind in the way this can be discerned on the feeling level: keeping the body still leads to painful feelings, but keeping the mind still leads to pleasant feelings. This remarkable contrast underscores the fact that it is simply much more meaningful to pursue wholesome happiness that originates from the mind than to pursue sensual happiness through the body.

Happiness is mental after all; it originates in the mind. Seeking happiness through the body is somewhat of a detour. It is much more straightforward to seek happiness through the mind by cultivating what is wholesome. It is not only more straightforward, it also stands a much greater chance of succeeding, because to do so accords with a natural tendency of a mind established in what is wholesome to give rise to joy. Last but not least, seeking happiness through bodily sense pleasures will keep us in continued bondage, but seeking happiness through establishing a wholesome condition of the mind will instead lead us onwards to liberation.

RIGHT VIEW

The realization of how our quest for happiness should best be directed is a matter of right view. Rightly viewing things provides the all-important orientation for pursuing a course of action that can indeed lead to lasting happiness.

Right view in the form of the four noble truths involves a shift from the first two truths, concerned with the recognition of *dukkha* and its cause, to the third and fourth truths. These are concerned with the recognition of the possibility of being free from *dukkha* and the way leading to such freedom, which is the noble eightfold path. This shift from the first and second to the third and fourth truths progresses from what is negative to what is positive. The two dimensions of contemplation of feelings just described involve a similar shift. This shift progresses from the realization that there is a subtle pain inherent in having a body, the alleviation of which is the motivating force behind much of our activities, to the recognition of the subtle joy of being in the present moment. Such parallelism supports a point made already above, in that contemplation of feeling offers a door to make right view by way of the four noble truths a matter of direct personal experience.

WORLDLY AND UNWORLDLY FEELINGS

In addition to the recognition of feelings as being pleasant, unpleasant, or neutral, the instructions in the *Satipaṭṭhāna-sutta* proceed to another distinction. The way this reads in the original gives me the impression that the entire instruction involves a two-step procedure. The first stage just requires recognizing the three basic affective tones. This has been the topic explored so far. Once some degree of familiarity with this type of practice has been acquired, the second stage comes into play. Here are the instructions:

> When feeling a worldly pleasant feeling, one knows: "I feel a worldly pleasant feeling"; *when feeling* an unworldly pleasant *feeling, one knows: "I feel an unworldly pleasant feeling"; when feeling* a worldly painful *feeling, one knows: "I feel a worldly painful feeling"; when feeling* an unworldly painful *feeling, one knows: "I feel an unworldly painful feeling"; when feeling* a worldly neutral *feeling, one knows: "I feel a worldly neutral feeling"*; when feeling an unworldly neutral feeling, one knows: "I feel an unworldly neutral feeling."

The distinction between worldly and unworldly involves Pāli terms that more literally translated distinguish between feelings related to the flesh (*āmisa*) and those not related to it. I take it that this distinction is meant to introduce an ethical dimension into the practice, which can function as a lead over to contemplation of mental states. In short, worldly feeling of the pleasant, unpleasant, and neutral types arises when the mind is with lust, anger, or delusion. Unworldly feeling of the same three affective types comes with a mind that is at least temporarily free from the influence of lust, anger, and delusion.

In a way it would have been more straightforward to speak just of wholesome and unwholesome feelings. Yet in its general usage the distinction between wholesome (*kusala*) and unwholesome (*akusala*) has a close relationship to intentions and intentional activities. Feelings, however, are not themselves a matter of intention. Whereas perceptions and volitional formations relate directly to intention and are amenable to mental training, feelings and consciousness are more the result of the situation created by perception and volitional formations. This basic difference could well be a reason why the discourses relate feeling and consciousness to the sense-object, whereas perception and volitional formations are related to the sense-door (Anālayo 2003: 204). In other words, feeling and consciousness are more on the receptive side of experience and thus less amenable to the direct influence of intention. This might explain why, instead of the more familiar distinction between what is wholesome and what is unwholesome, for contemplation of feelings the less common distinction between what is worldly and what is unworldly has been employed.

The introduction of the distinction between worldly and unworldly feelings can be further appreciated in the light of the Buddha's own progress to awakening. According to the *Mahāsaccaka-sutta*, during the period of his asceticism the future Buddha experienced excruciating pain, yet such pain did not overwhelm his mind. Similarly, when cultivating the absorptions during the time before his awakening he was able to experience the joy and happiness of deep concentration without his mind being overwhelmed by it (MN 36; Anālayo 2017c: 92).

In the case of the Buddha, ensuring that the mind did not become overwhelmed by feelings was an integral part of his constant monitoring of what he was doing. Such monitoring was necessary, since he was uncertain about what path and practice would lead him to awakening. Therefore he had to keep monitoring what was happening, in order to be able to assess whether what he was doing resulted in progress towards the final goal of liberation. I take it that such monitoring, in itself perhaps just the result of his practising without the guidance of a teacher, turned out to be so beneficial that, when teaching others, he decided to give it a prominent position in the form of *satipaṭṭhāna* meditation.

By monitoring the impact of feelings on the mind in particular, he developed a distinct assessment of the nature of feelings. The average attitude of the untrained mind is to pursue pleasure and avoid pain. Asceticism is based on the recognition that this attitude leads to bondage. The alternative advocated by followers of asceticism is just the opposite: pursue pain and avoid pleasure. Out of his own experience with both sensual indulgence in his youth and self-inflicted pain during his asceticism, the Buddha went beyond both attitudes. He realized that some forms of pleasure are commendable and others should be avoided. Again, some forms of pain are commendable and others should be avoided (MN 70; Anālayo 2017c: 74ff). This understanding involves a significant shift of perspective, where feelings are evaluated according to their repercussions rather than their affective tone. The discovery of this different perspective could well be what informs the distinction introduced in the instructions in the *Satipaṭṭhāna-sutta* between worldly and unworldly feelings.

The *Cūḷavedalla-sutta* builds on this basic distinction between a feeling's affective tone and its repercussions. The discourse presents the first absorption as an example of pleasant feelings that do not stimulate sensual desire. The fourth absorption exemplifies neutral feelings that do not stimulate ignorance. Wishing for liberation exemplifies unpleasant feelings that do not stimulate aversion (MN 44; Anālayo 2013: 127f).

In this way, pleasant feelings of a worldly type are those related to sensuality. Those of an unworldly type are the joy and happiness of deep concentration. Even more unworldly than that, however, is the happiness of liberation (SN 36.29; Anālayo 2003: 158n9). The principle behind this type of presentation is that worldly pleasant feelings are those that lead to an increase of sensual desire. Unworldly pleasant feelings instead lead to a decrease of sensual desire. The happiness of deep concentration does indeed diminish interest in sensuality. A mind that is fully liberated is forever free from sensual desire. Consequently the joy of liberation is the supreme type of unworldly pleasant feeling.

Unpleasant feelings of a worldly type would be those arising on being deprived of sensual pleasures. Regarding unpleasant feelings of the unworldly type, the *Cūḷavedalla-sutta* describes how such feelings arise due to wishing for liberation. This goes to show that there is nothing in principle wrong with the wish or aspiration to be liberated. The recognition of not having yet reached the goal can be useful in stirring up the energy required for further progress. However, this needs to be handled properly in order not to go overboard. When such aspiration leads to depression and excessive frustration, it can turn into an obstacle.

Related to the topic of unpleasant feelings that pertain to the unworldly type are occasions when we recognize that we have failed to live up to our own standards of conduct and behaviour. It can be quite helpful to remind ourselves that such experiences are an integral part of the path. Learning to bear with patience the unpleasant feelings arisen at such times counters the natural tendency to avoid such displeasure by simply ignoring our own shortcomings. If this tendency is allowed to take its course, the final result could well be that we train ourselves to pretend that we are better than we really are. This would indeed be an obstacle for further progress. Honest acknowledgement of our own defilements and shortcomings is an indispensable foundation for being able to do something about them. Unworldly feelings of the unpleasant type clearly have their place. This does not mean that we should indulge in self-deprecation. As with all the other *satipaṭṭhāna* exercises, the task is to keep balanced. The tool for achieving such balance is always mindfulness. Mindful observation offers us feedback as soon as we are off balance.

Neutral feelings of the worldly type could be when we are at least momentarily satiated by sensuality and our interest in further indulgence is no longer stimulated, at least for the time being. Think of having eaten your fill and being offered another delicious dish. The feelings that arise at this time will be substantially different from the feelings experienced when being offered the same delicious dish at a time when we are really hungry. The key point here is that the neutral reaction is not the outcome of insight, but rather a type of indifference that remains within the domain of ignorance.

A prominent example of neutral unworldly feelings would be the fourth absorption. To the same category belong other neutral feelings experienced during meditation or else as the outcome of insight leading to equanimity.

The contrast between worldly and unworldly neutral feelings could also be viewed from the perspective of the *Saḷāyatanavibhaṅga-sutta* (MN 137; Anālayo 2003: 172 and 2013: 131). This discourse describes a hierarchy of feelings to be cultivated, where the neutral hedonic tone experienced with the cultivation of insight stands out as the supreme one. In view of the tendency of neutral feelings to give rise to boredom, due to their bland nature, appreciating the superiority of this particular type of neutral feeling can help to sustain the momentum of meditation practice during retreat periods. In other words, it is in a way natural that at times the mind finds intensive meditation less entertaining and goes seeking something else to stimulate interest. Yet from the viewpoint of the teachings it is precisely the neutral feelings experienced when seeing the impermanent nature of phenomena that form the very acme in the experience of feelings; it is precisely this type of experience that is to be cultivated.

IMPERMANENCE

Having practised contemplation of feelings for some time, another feature becomes more and more prominent, which is the changing nature of feelings. Where we earlier noticed that a feeling of a particular hedonic tone had arisen, sooner or later we find that it has passed away. With this constant arising and passing away, in a way every feeling is a messenger of impermanence. Feelings are so ephemeral, they are like bubbles on the surface of water during rain (SN 22.95; Anālayo 2003: 206). They constantly keep arising and passing away. Their impermanent nature makes feelings a convenient tool for the cultivation of deepening insight into impermanence. Through the present exercise, such insight becomes a palpable and directly felt experience. We *feel* impermanence. Feeling impermanence makes it indubitably clear that pleasure and pain do not last forever. Experiencing this directly for ourselves gradually erodes the tendency for feelings to trigger strong reactions.

Appreciation of the changing nature of feelings does require an intentional effort. In a way, with the previous body contemplation of a corpse in decay the truth of impermanence can hardly be missed. But with feelings as well as with mental states, impermanence needs to be actively encouraged in order to proceed with the practice in accordance with the stipulation in the refrain of the *Satipaṭṭhāna-sutta*. According to the refrain, the task is contemplating the nature of arising and of passing away.

Once we are established in that felt sense of impermanence, thoughts no longer need to be seen as a distraction from contemplation of feelings. As long as we stay rooted in awareness of the whole body and attuned to this directly felt sense of change, thoughts can be left as they are. There is no need to force them out of the mind in order to be able to contemplate feelings. If we simply leave them as they are, without getting involved with them, they will gradually lose their power to carry the mind away. Eventually they can just come to be part of a comprehensive experience of impermanence.

The same comprehensive experience of impermanence continues from sitting to walking meditation. During the actual walking, attention can be paid to the sensations related to this activity. These could be the touch sensations on the soles of the feet, the sensations in the leg, or the whole body. In being aware of these various sensations, their impermanent nature can be given special attention. In this way the felt sense of change becomes a continuous practice.

Feelings are like winds that come from different directions (SN 36.12; Anālayo 2003: 160 and 2013: 132). Just as it would be meaningless to contend with the vicissitudes of the weather, similarly it is meaningless to contend with the vicissitudes of feelings. The best attitude is to simply let both feelings and winds pass by. Both can be left to run their natural course in the knowledge that they will change anyway.

> Cultivate the mind
> Like the empty sky,
> Allow feelings' wind
> Simply to pass by.

In terms of the wheel simile, the contribution made by contemplation of feeling to the hub of the wheel is to root mindfulness in the body even more firmly by attending directly to the felt sense of the body and by combining that with the joy of being in the present moment. Moreover, this felt sense of the presence of the body comes with a built-in pointer to the fact of change. The contribution made to the rim of the wheel is a deepening sense of non-attachment.

It is futile to cling to feelings that are so ephemeral and constantly changing. The tendency to react to feelings by giving rise to craving is undermined and progressively weakened. In particular the quest for sensual pleasures through the body discloses its meaninglessness. It is not only pointless, but even outright dangerous. This danger becomes particularly evident when the body becomes sick and is in pain. To the degree that we have become attached to bodily feelings during previous pursuits of sensuality, to that degree we will be afflicted by bodily feelings when disease manifests.

OPEN PRACTICE

Based on the insight cultivated with the three body contemplations and the input provided by mindfully exploring feelings, we move on to an undirected mode of practice. Rooted in whole-body awareness and with the continuity of that felt sense of impermanence, we open up to the present moment in whatever way it unfolds. We are aware that "there is feeling" (*atthi vedanā*), which can take the form of experiencing our rootedness in awareness of the whole body through the medium of feelings. In this way we keep proceeding on the path to freedom from all unwholesome reactivity in relation to feelings.

When we notice that the mind has got distracted, smilingly we recognize that the mind has wandered away, and then try to identify the feeling tone. What was the predominant affective tone of the thought, experience, memory, or fantasy that led to the distraction? Was it pleasant, unpleasant, or neutral? Such recognition of the predominant feeling tone can offer support for contemplation of the mind, the next *satipaṭṭhāna*, in particular in relation to the need to discern manifestations of lust, anger, and delusion. I will return to this relationship between the second and the third *satipaṭṭhāna*s in the next chapter.

From an insight perspective, an important contribution made by contemplation of feeling is to offer a direct and personal realization of the principle of dependent arising. In a way the final link of dependent arising has already become evident with the previous contemplation of death. By facing death, we trained ourselves not to react with the sorrow and grief that usually come intertwined with the experience of death. That type of training implicitly points to craving and clinging, namely to the craving not to be affected by death and the clinging to life.

Building on awareness of the mortality of the body as an outstanding manifestation of *dukkha*, the present exercise turns to a crucial juncture in the series of links that lead up to the dependent arising of *dukkha*. This is the arising of craving in dependence on feeling. The distinct push exerted on the mind by feeling makes it palpably evident why the link between feeling and craving is of such importance. It is at this juncture in dependent arising that mindfulness can make a world of difference.

SUMMARY

The three types of feeling can be explored with the help of body scans, which should lead over to a comprehensive awareness of any feeling, including those mental ones that do not have a clearly noticeable bodily component. Noticing the push of feelings for some reaction to take place discloses their conditioning impact on the mind. Sustained contemplation reveals the body to be a recurrent source of painful feelings, whereas the mind established in the present moment yields a subtle type of pleasant feeling. Any feeling can serve as an entry door into the direct experience of impermanence.

VII

MIND

The fifth spoke in the wheel of practice presented here, which corresponds to the third *satipaṭṭhāna*, is contemplation of mental states. The first part of the instructions given in the *Satipaṭṭhāna-sutta* proceeds as follows (MN 10):

> One knows a mind with lust to be "a mind with lust"; or one knows a mind without lust to be "a mind without lust"; *or one knows a mind* with anger *to be "a mind with anger"; or one knows a mind* without anger *to be "a mind without anger"; or one knows a mind* with delusion *to be "a mind with delusion"; or one knows a mind* without delusion *to be "a mind without delusion"; or one knows a* contracted *mind to be "a contracted mind"; or one knows a* distracted *mind to be "a distracted mind".*

Although in what follows I will be taking up in detail the individual states of mind mentioned above, at the outset I would like to note that the main thrust of the present contemplation can be summarized as a continuous inward monitoring with the question: "how is the mind?" Whatever may happen outside, which is where all our attention usually goes, becomes secondary from this perspective. What really counts is how the mind reacts to it. This is what we need to keep noticing. It is such knowing of our own mind that is the chief concern of the present *satipaṭṭhāna*, for the purpose of which the actual mental states listed serve as aids or exemplifications.

LUST, ANGER, AND DELUSION

The first three states of mind in the instructions above take up the presence and absence of lust, anger, and delusion. I suggest giving particular emphasis to these three during actual practice. Whenever a distraction occurs, it could either involve some form of desire or lust, or else be related to the presence of some degree of aversion or anger. The third alternative is when the mind is just ambling around, a condition of distraction not prominently coloured by lust or anger. This condition of the mind can be considered a manifestation of delusion. Needless to say, delusion also underlies lust and anger. But for practical purposes, it seems to me preferable to employ this category in such a way that it can be used as a complement to the first two detrimental states mentioned in the instructions.

Familiarity with the presence or absence of lust, anger, and delusion within will in turn facilitate recognizing the same externally, when such presence or absence manifests in others. Such recognition can rely on facial expression, tone of voice, and bodily posture as pointers to the mental condition of another (Anālayo 2003: 97 and 2017a: 37n39).

The employment of these three categories helps to build a bridge from the preceding contemplation of feelings, in particular in relation to feelings of a worldly type. When lust is present in the mind, chances are that it comes accompanied by worldly pleasant feelings. Similarly, when anger arises, chances are that such arising is accompanied by worldly painful feelings. When delusion arises in turn, chances are that worldly neutral feelings are present in the mind.

Working with this relationship can offer considerable support for recognizing the arising of these detrimental states. Such recognition has to do with a basic task required by contemplation of states of mind. This task is to see through a particular train of thought and its related associations in order to discern the underlying mental current. For mindful recognition of our present mental state, the requirement is above all a clear recognition without getting involved in the details of whatever train of thought and related associations are taking place. Since it is often precisely these details that get us hooked and caught up in a particular chain of thoughts, achieving such recognition is more easily said than done. Recognizing the feeling tone of our current experience offers help for this task. It grounds awareness in the affective reality of the present moment and thereby draws attention to our subjective involvement in whatever is happening. In this way we learn to attend to the baseline condition of the mind rather than to the details of particular thoughts.

This is of considerable importance, since human beings are quite able to remain immersed in their thoughts while at the same time completely ignoring the baseline emotional condition of the corresponding state of mind. History abounds with examples of incredibly cruel actions that have had their basis in the fascination exerted by a particular political or religious ideal, leading to a thorough dissociation from basic qualities like kindness and compassion (at times in combination with relegating to some higher authority the responsibility for the harm inflicted on others). Other examples of no less atrocious events show the opposite side of the same coin, when wallowing in emotions takes place in complete dissociation from the rational capacities of the mind. The present practice works against the grain of the tendency of dissociation, based on the groundwork preparation of embodied awareness and clear recognition of the feeling tone of experience.

This in turn brings out the significance of the three *satipaṭṭhāna*s explored so far and the importance of practising them in conjunction rather than in isolation from each other. It is precisely through the preparatory work done so far in the somatic and affective domain that the present *satipaṭṭhāna* acquires its full potential. Mindfulness cultivated in this way can be visualized as opening up the communication channels between these different domains. It offers a point of integration of the rational and emotional dimensions of ourselves. This takes place by giving each an equal hearing in such a way that both can make their contribution to a complete assessment of a particular situation and to finding the appropriate response to it. In this way, intuition and reasoning come to a point of balance, based on the support provided by mindfulness. This results from the dynamics of practice underlying the first three *satipaṭṭhānas*.

The specific contribution made by the third *satipaṭṭhāna* in this respect is proper identification of the actual condition of our state of mind as a direct approach to honest recognition and the taking of responsibility for what happens within. In practical terms, this can take the form of a regular check-in to see how the mind is doing right now. Shifting from the ingrained tendency of giving all attention to the objects of experience, we instead direct some attention to the repercussions of the experiencing of those objects in the inner domain of our mind.

In a way we are so used to focusing on what is taking place outside or what we are engaged in doing that our mental range of vision has come to resemble the restricted range of vision of our physical eyes. The basic pattern is to give all attention to what is right in front of us. Or else, if something really strong comes up in the emotional domain, the narrow beam of focus shifts to that; we turn around, as it were, and all else is completely forgotten.

But such a restricted range of mental vision is a habit rather than a necessity. The mind is not by nature limited in a manner comparable to human eyes. Actualizing this potential requires stepping back from too narrow a focus of attention and allowing our awareness to become more comprehensive. In this way we learn to apperceive the *how* of experience alongside its *what*. At the subjective level we discern the mental repercussions of what is taking place, a discerning that does not in any way inhibit our ability to perceive and interact with what is taking place outside. Indeed, the resultant breadth of mind improves both our taking in of information and our ability to deal with whatever has occurred in an appropriate manner.

A basic training in expanding the range of our mental vision has been introduced gradually through the previous *satipaṭṭhāna* exercises, where with contemplation of the anatomical parts and the elements we already went beyond the average perception of the body, concerned predominantly with its surface appearance, by attending to its more internal aspects. With contemplation of feeling we learned to turn inwards from having felt the body to becoming aware of that which feels the body. Now the task is to continue further in the same inward direction by attending to that which knows the body and that which knows feelings.

In the example of holding this book in our hands, used in the last chapter, attention proceeded from the touch sensation of the book to feeling the hands that were touching the book. In line with the overall thrust of the present *satipaṭṭhāna*, attention can now turn further inwards to that which knows the experience of holding this book in our hands: the mind.

The resultant broadening of the scope of meditative attention by including the actual state of our own mind is of fundamental importance for *satipaṭṭhāna* meditation. It lays the foundation for the present and the next *satipaṭṭhāna*, contemplation of dharmas concerned with the hindrances and the awakening factors. Cultivating the ability to monitor what goes on within, to recognize clearly the condition of our own mind, is indispensable for being able to explore fully the potential of these two out of the four *satipaṭṭhānas*.

Actually in a way the same is required for all *satipaṭṭhāna* meditation, in that we need to monitor how what we do affects our mind. This became clear already with the first exercise, contemplation of anatomical parts. The story of the suicide of monastics due to unbalanced practice of this contemplation serves as a strong warning of the dangers of not keeping an eye on what happens in the mind (see above p. 60).

The required turning inwards to check in on the actual condition of the mind is somewhat like reading an interesting book in the awareness that we soon have an appointment with a good friend. While reading, we keep the passage of time in mind. We might regularly glance at a watch just to make sure we do not miss the time for the meeting. This need not be something stressful or disturbing, but can simply be a relaxed way of keeping the passage of time in our peripheral awareness while nevertheless enjoying the book. Similarly, peripheral awareness can in a relaxed manner keep an eye on how things are unfolding within, monitoring the condition of our mind.

In the context of an account of the gradual path, contemplation of the mental states of others finds illustration in looking into a

mirror (DN 2; Anālayo 2014a: 80). This illustrates well what the present practice is about, but in relation to ourselves: holding up the mirror of mindfulness within, in order to see clearly the reflection of our own state of mind as it is right now. This act of introspectively checking the condition of our own mind could be compared to keeping an eye on the rear-view mirror while driving a car. This helps us to have the whole traffic situation in view, rather than seeing only what is happening in front. In the same way, we look into the rear-view mirror within to see how the mind relates to whatever is happening. Again, comparable to using a mirror to ascertain whether our bodily appearance is clean or dirty, similarly we look into the mirror of mindfulness in order to ascertain the condition of our mental appearance.

Just as we ask others: "How are you?", so we now keep asking ourselves: "How is the mind?" Expressed in terms of the three categories of contemplation of the mind mentioned above: "how is the mind, is it with lust or without lust, with anger or without anger, with delusion or without delusion?"

Mindfulness of feelings is of particular help in recognizing unwholesome thoughts before they have acquired full force. As mentioned in the previous chapter, such recognition at an initial stage in the building up of unwholesome thoughts makes it possible to nip these in the bud. At an early stage, the detrimental thoughts and associations are not yet in full swing. The degree of our identification is not yet as strong as it will eventually become if they continue. This makes it easier to step out of the thought, to let it go and change the course of the mind.

Imagine a snowball rolling down a hill. It will be easier to change its course or stop it if we catch it close to the top of the hill. Once it has moved farther down and become bigger and faster, it will be much more difficult to intercept. The course of the mind is similar.

Activating this potential requires the willingness to look at our own shortcomings. This is another topic already broached in the previous chapter, the importance of learning to bear with patience the recognition of any failure to live up to our own standards. The feelings experienced at such times are most likely feelings of the unpleasant type. Such feelings take on an unworldly dimension because they have the potential to lead us forward on the path. Self-deception as a means to avoid the displeasure of seeing our own shortcomings stands diametrically opposed to the whole thrust of progress on the path of *satipaṭṭhāna* meditation.

The importance of honest and clear recognition comes out in the *Anaṅgaṇa-sutta* (MN 5; Anālayo 2013: 160f). The discourse places emphasis on the importance of clearly acknowledging the presence of a defilement as an indispensable prerequisite for being able to do something about it. If recognition is not there, the foundation for emerging from this detrimental condition is lacking.

THE ABSENCE OF DEFILEMENTS

The same *Anaṅgaṇa-sutta* similarly gives importance to recognizing the absence of a defilement. This principle also underlies the instructions for contemplation of the mind in the *Satipaṭṭhāna-sutta*. After mentioning the need to recognize a mental state with lust, for example, the instructions continue: "one knows a mind without lust to be 'a mind without lust'." The same holds for anger and delusion. Absence of lust, anger, and delusion is as much a matter to be known as their presence. In this way, what is absent becomes a presence through attending to its absence.

The need to recognize both presence and absence is also implicit in the instruction in the refrain to contemplate arising and passing away. Having noticed that lust or anger has arisen, for example, the task is to notice similarly when subsequently lust and anger have passed away. This need applies also to the mental states listed under the two contemplations of dharmas concerned with the hindrances and the awakening factors. Throughout awareness that a particular mental state has arisen finds its complement in awareness of its eventual passing away. The two in combination make it clear that it is indeed the nature of any mental state to arise and pass away.

It is of considerable importance that the need, evident in the list of mental states as well as in the refrain, to direct attention to the passing away of a defiled mental state is not overlooked. The task of mindfulness is not only to draw attention to the presence of a defilement. It similarly involves giving attention to the absence of a defilement. We can savour the condition of the mind at such times, get a feel for its texture, and familiarize ourselves with it. We can experience for ourselves how much more pleasant such a condition is when compared to a defiled state of mind. Familiarizing ourselves with the difference between the presence and the absence of a defilement in terms of the texture and flavour of the mind will make it intuitively clear why the latter is preferable to the former.

The mind is somewhat like a child or a puppy. It needs to be encouraged to do what we want it to do. Imagine calling a puppy or a child by its name and then hitting it, because earlier it did something wrong. Do this a few times and the puppy or the child will learn not to come when called. Similarly, if we keep hitting ourselves by becoming frustrated and upset every time a defilement manifests in the mind, we run the risk of actually training the mind in such a way that eventually it no longer recognizes a defilement.

If we want the puppy or the child to come when its name is called, we had better give it some reward. Why not reward ourselves for a state of mind that is undefiled? Rejoicing in the absence of defilements is a powerful tool that will make for swift progress on the path to permanent freedom from defilements.

This does not mean turning a blind eye to defilements. These should be honestly recognized, but ideally without aversion. It is possible to realize that a defilement is in the mind and smile. We smile at the tendency of the mind to do the opposite of what we want it to do. We smile in the knowledge that we are walking a gradual path and that it would be unreasonable to expect that, as soon as we sit down to meditate, the mind just does what we want.

In actual practice, given the previous four contemplations, chances are that at this stage of *satipaṭṭhāna* meditation the type of mind we are experiencing is at least momentarily without lust, without anger, and perhaps even without deluded distractions. It is good to recognize this. Such recognition can in turn lead to rejoicing in the condition of temporary freedom from lust, anger, or delusion. Although the roots of the defilements are still in the mind, at least these defilements are not manifesting on the surface level. This much is sufficient cause for rejoicing. By rejoicing in this way, we accord to wholesome types of happiness the place they deserve within the gradual path to liberation. The importance of joy and happiness of this type is clearly recognized in the early discourses. According to the *Kandaraka-sutta*, for example, progress on the gradual path involves a progressive refinement of non-sensual types of happiness (MN 51; Anālayo 2003: 167).

Intentionally arousing joy when realizing that the mind is temporarily free will go a long way in strengthening the tendency of the mind to remain in the realm of what is wholesome. It also serves to provide inspiration for the practice.

Cultivating a habit of rejoicing in wholesome conditions of the mind will make meditation so much more attractive and turn it into something that we look forward to, instead of being something done out of a sense of obligation. Moreover, it also offers a foretaste of the final goal. The final goal is purification of the mind from all defilements. Instead of remaining an abstract concept, through recognition of the pleasant condition of the mind that is temporarily free from defilements we can have a direct experience of the aim of our practice.

Such joy it can be
When the mind is free
Even if only
Temporarily.

CONTRACTED AND DISTRACTED

Besides mentioning lust, anger, and delusion, the first part of the instructions distinguishes between a contracted and a distracted state of mind. The implications of a contracted mind are open to question (Anālayo 2003: 178). One mode of interpretation would be to assume that in this case both mental states are detrimental. On this interpretation, a contracted mental condition could be the outcome of sloth-and-torpor or else the result of becoming narrow-minded or contracting mentally out of fear or aversion. Distraction could then refer to any scattered condition of the mind.

Alternatively, this pair could be interpreted in line with the general pattern in the listing of mental states in the *Satipaṭṭhāna-sutta* as involving a contrast between a positive and a negative state, or between a superior and an inferior mental condition. Following this mode of interpretation, the present pair would involve the difference between a mind that is not distracted, in the sense of being collected, and a mind that is distracted. Although to my mind the actual terminology makes the first interpretation more probable, I would leave it up to the individual practitioner to decide which of these two interpretations appears more meaningful for actual practice.

Whichever interpretation we adopt, there is no doubt that this part of the instructions requires identifying a condition of mental distraction for what it is. The challenge here is that distractions can at times be rather subtle and often also quite enticing. For this reason it is particularly important to stick to the element of mindful recognition. This requires withstanding the temptation to let ourselves be carried away by the (at least momentarily) pleasurable condition of a distracted mind. For genuine progress to liberation even subtle distraction needs to be acknowledged for what it is: a condition of the mind that diverts our attention and therefore is not conducive to our meditative growth.

HIGHER STATES OF MIND

The remaining four pairs in the instructions are less concerned with defilements. Here is the relevant passage:

> *Or one knows a mind that has* become great *to be "a mind that has become great"; or one knows a mind that has* not become great *to be "a mind that has not become great"; or one knows a* surpassable *mind to be "a surpassable mind"; or one knows an* unsurpassable *mind to be "an unsurpassable mind"; or one knows a* concentrated *mind to be "a concentrated mind"; or one knows a* not concentrated *mind to be "a not concentrated mind"; or one knows a* liberated *mind to be "a liberated mind";* or one knows a not liberated mind to be "a not liberated mind."

The four terms mentioned in the second half of the instructions refer to a mind that has become:

- great (or not),
- surpassable (or not),
- concentrated (or not),
- liberated (or not).

The qualification "great" employed for the first of these is also used for the cultivation of the *brahmavihāras* (Anālayo 2003: 179 and 2015: 55f). In a more general sense, this category could be taken to point to an opening of the heart. In addition, a mind that has become great could also come about through other modes of cultivating tranquillity. Yet I suggest including these rather under the header of the third term, the mind that is "concentrated", in order to be able to associate distinct meanings with these different categories when applied in actual practice.

The second pair mentioned in the instruction concerns the mind that is either surpassable or unsurpassable. Within the realm of absorption attainment, an unsurpassed condition of the mind will be reached with the attainment of the highest absorption (Anālayo 2003: 179). In a general sense, however, I would take this pair to point to the ability to recognize whether a particular meditative experience can be taken further. In other words, whatever is happening right now in our meditation, does it have the potential to lead to something higher? Or have we already arrived at what is possible within this particular sitting or course of meditation practice? Moreover, the category of a surpassable mind would also fit the case of the hindrances, which can and should indeed be surpassed.

The third term mentions a mind that is concentrated or not concentrated, which could fruitfully be understood to refer to the monitoring of mindfulness required for the deepening of tranquillity and the eventual attainment of absorption. Mindfulness is in fact present throughout absorption attainment, where it becomes particularly prominent with the third and fourth absorptions (Anālayo 2017a: 150).

Relevant to the present as well as the two preceding categories is the analytical attitude so prominent in early Buddhist meditation theory (Anālayo 2003: 180f). Instead of getting carried away by a particular meditation experience, the task is to recognize the degree of concentration achieved and what mental factors are present in this state of mind. In other words, when during practice the mind tends towards deeper levels of concentration, we simply accompany such natural development with mindful monitoring. Deeper states of tranquillity are an integral part of the path, as long as their impermanent and ultimately unsatisfactory nature is clearly understood and as long as identification with, or even reification of, such experiences is avoided.

The last pair in the *Satipaṭṭhāna-sutta*'s instructions distinguishes between a mind that is liberated and one that is not liberated. In the highest sense, this would refer to the retrospective knowledge of an arahant who realizes that the mind has been fully liberated (Anālayo 2003: 180). The same term could also be related to the cultivation of tranquillity, in the sense of the mind being liberated from obstructions to absorption attainment. Since absorption has already been covered with the label of the concentrated mind, I prefer to use the present label instead in relation to the cultivation of insight. My suggestion would be to check whether the mind has been at least temporarily liberated from selfing. Can we meditate without the ego making the front page, without constructing the self-referential sense of a meditator who appropriates the meditative experience as something to be owned and possessed? Can the conceit of an I be allowed to go into abeyance during our actual practice?

In this way, according to the mode of interpretation presented here, the four categories introduced in this part of the discourse could be employed with the following practical implications: the mind that has become great (or not) would reflect an opening of the heart, such as reached with the *brahmavihāras*. The surpassable (or unsurpassable) mind would point to the recognition that meditation can be taken further. The mind that has become concentrated (or not) would involve monitoring the deepening of mental tranquillity to reach absorption. The mind that has become liberated (or not) would reflect the absence of identifications and the sense of a self.

Needless to say, these are just my suggestions. Practitioners should feel free to adjust these in line with their personal understanding and preferences. Whatever interpretation we prefer, when overwhelmed by a hindrance the mind is clearly narrow and not great, as well as neither concentrated nor liberated. As already mentioned above, it is quite definitely surpassable. The task of the next *satipaṭṭhāna* is precisely to explore the conditions that help us to emerge from a hindrance, to surpass it and thereby allow the mind to become greater, more concentrated, and more liberated than it was when the hindrance was still present.

In a way, qualifications of the mind as great, concentrated, liberated, and even unsurpassable, listed in the instructions for the present *satipaṭṭhāna*, reflect the role of mindfulness in monitoring the progress of our meditation. A crucial element to be kept in mind for such monitoring, which can range from identifying and overcoming a hindrance to the experience of deep levels of concentration and insight, is that progress in *satipaṭṭhāna* meditation is not just about having special experiences. Special experiences certainly have their place, but they are not the goal itself. The goal is rather inner transformation. Even the experience of an absorption or a stage of awakening has its true value in the extent to which it produces lasting inner transformation. Meditation practice should result in an improvement in the way we are, how we relate to others, and how we deal with outer circumstances. Such internal changes are more important than appropriating spectacular experiences as markers of our meditative expertise.

In this context it may also be relevant to note that in early Buddhist thought the distinction between path and fruit differs from the way these terms are used in later traditions. Path and fruit are not just two mind-moments immediately following each other. Instead, the path covers the whole trajectory of even years of practice and its fruit is to be found in personal transformation, in the eradication of fetters and defilements. This invests the actual meditative experience with somewhat less weight than is the case when one is influenced by the perspective on path and fruit in later tradition.

OPENING OF THE HEART

Of particular importance in relation to such personal transformation, I believe, is a genuine opening of the heart to the qualities of kindness and compassion. In my personal view, such opening of the heart is a better measuring rod for progress in our practice than having extraordinary experiences. In order to encourage this dimension of practice and also as a way of mirroring the Buddha's own unswerving quest for awakening, I suggest introducing a formal element of setting our intention at the beginning of each formal sitting. This could be an aspiration like: "May I progress on the path to liberation, for my own benefit and for the benefit of others."

Evoking such an aspiration affords an opportunity to bring in the path factor of right intention. Needless to say, for *satipaṭṭhāna* meditation to yield its full potential, it needs to be situated within the context of the noble eightfold path.

Formulating our motivation at the outset of formal meditation provides a reference point for the course of our practice. It clearly sets the direction in which we wish to go. Including an altruistic disposition in this type of reference point is particularly beneficial. It not only encourages the opening of the heart to compassion, but also provides strength during challenging times. Simply said, we are not just practising for ourselves; we are also practising for the sake of others. Awareness of this external dimension of our meditation practice makes it easier to withstand any onslaught of doubt and frustration. Missing out on the compassionate dimension runs the risk of turning the practice of meditation into a self-centred enterprise. Meditating only for our own benefit makes it more difficult to sustain the practice in times of difficulty.

Strictly speaking, compassion is not part of *satipaṭṭhāna* meditation. It falls under the path factor of right intention in the form of intending to avoid what is harmful for others (and ourselves). Although not explicitly mentioned in the *Satipaṭṭhāna-sutta*, compassion has been an underlying current through the previous exercises.

Contemplation of the anatomical parts directly counters the tendency for sensual lust to get out of control, which can lead to horrible things like rape or child abuse. This is the very opposite of kindness and compassion.

Contemplation of the elements has made it indubitably clear that we are an inseparable part of outside nature. Discrimination against others due to their race or physical build becomes meaningless once we realize that we are all made up of the same elements. Such a realization makes it easier for us to have compassion and cultivate a genuine concern for the environment.

Recollection of death encourages a willingness to forgive and apologize. Time is just too short to carry a grudge or unnecessarily prolong a conflict. Moreover, having learned to face our own mortality enables us to be of real assistance to others who are dying or mourning.

With the foundation laid by these three body contemplations, contemplation of feeling naturally leads to an increased sensitivity to what happens on the affective level. Based on this groundwork, contemplation of the mind in its internal (and even more so in its external) dimension can become an occasion for a genuine opening of the heart. In the image of the lotus that I like to use to illustrate *satipaṭṭhāna* meditation (see above p. 39 and below p. 208), compassion is like the seeds found inside this lotus.

SKILFUL USE OF LABELS

In terms of actual practice, it is noteworthy that the instructions for contemplation of mental states, as well as the instructions in other parts of the discourse, involve the use of labels. It is certainly not the case that *satipaṭṭhāna* meditation takes place in the absence of concepts. This relates back to the topic of the coexistence of mindfulness with concepts (see above p. 7ff) and the relationship between a map and reality (see above p. 53f). In the present case, the instructions are formulated in such a way that they imply some degree of mental verbalization. The reference to a mind with anger, for example, is followed by the particle *iti*, which in Pāli marks the end of a quotation. Clearly the implication is that an explicit conceptual label should be employed in order to sharpen clarity of recognition, almost as if mentally saying to ourselves: "anger".

At the same time, however, *satipaṭṭhāna* meditation is not about ceaseless labelling. The use of a label for the sake of clear recognition is best followed by just dwelling in awareness of the texture of the mind, savouring its condition and flavour. In this way, briefly bringing up a label can function in a similar way to quickly checking a compass when hiking in order to make sure we are still going in the right direction. That much is often enough, without any need to keep checking the compass continuously and also pulling out the road map to study it in detail over and over again.

A relevant passage for appreciating the need to beware of excessive thinking activity can be found in the *Dvedhāvitakka-sutta* (MN 19; Anālayo 2013: 146ff). The discourse describes how, during the time before his awakening, the future Buddha divided his thoughts into two types: those that are unwholesome and those that are wholesome. This basic distinction underlies the first states of mind listed in the *Satipaṭṭhāna-sutta*. Unlike the case of unwholesome thoughts, with their wholesome counterparts the future Buddha saw no danger in having such thoughts. Yet he also saw that excessive thinking will tire body and mind and become an obstruction to the deepening of concentration.

The same applies to *satipaṭṭhāna*. The use of labelling is a helpful tool, but it should not be overused. Excessive labelling will tire body and mind and become an obstruction to the deepening of our practice. In view of this I like to suggest a simplification of the list of mental states given in the instructions for the present *satipaṭṭhāna*. In a way, recognition of any of the mental states mentioned in the instructions relies on the presence of mindfulness, which in the mode of practice I am presenting here is in particular an embodied form of mindfulness. For this reason it seems to me sensible to use the simple recognition of whether such mindfulness continues to be present or has been lost as a summary of contemplation of the mind. Such a summary can even be employed at times when bringing in more labels risks tiring the mind and disturbing the flow of meditative practice. Based on this succinct mode, at other times more labels can be brought in, as appropriate.

A mind in which mindfulness is well established has a distinct flavour and texture, such as being open, receptive, flexible, alive, centred, clear, and calm. Familiarizing ourselves with how our mind actually feels when we are mindful helps us to recognize this condition even without any need for labelling. It also enables us to realize quickly when we are about to incur a loss of mindfulness, when the mind just begins to close down, becoming a bit less receptive, slightly contracted, somewhat automatic rather than being really alive to what is taking place, no longer fully centred, somewhat unclear, and not as calm as earlier. Noticing such markers of an impending loss of mindfulness makes it easier to react swiftly and take the appropriate measures in order to become again properly grounded in the presence of mindfulness.

Being well grounded in the presence of mindfulness is an indispensable requirement for progress in meditation. Mindfulness serves to monitor the arousing and balancing of the absorption factors when cultivating tranquillity and of the awakening factors when cultivating insight. In both cases, without a grounding in mindfulness the practice will not unfold its full potential. Hence any time we invest in familiarizing ourselves with the distinct flavour and texture of a mind in which mindfulness is well established, learning how to foster such a mental condition and beware of its loss, is an investment of time that will benefit our meditation practice in many ways.

OPEN PRACTICE

The same grounding continues when shifting to open awareness. Familiarity with the texture of the mind in which mindfulness is established facilitates our being aware that "there is the mind". Rooted in whole-body awareness we are aware of the impermanent nature of phenomena in whatever way these manifest in the present moment. The simple recognition of whether we are still mentally on track serves as a continuous element during our *satipaṭṭhāna* meditation. The distinct sense of the embodied presence of mindfulness can become a baseline for the third *satipaṭṭhāna*, in the sense of enabling a continuous mode of contemplation of the mind. Such baseline practice in turn provides a solid foundation for being able to recognize any of the other mental states, listed in the discourse, as and when they manifest. In this way, just as the continuous presence of proprioceptive awareness can alert us to any loss of bodily balance, so the continuous presence of embodied mindfulness can alert us to any loss of mental balance.

When substantial distractions occur, the first three categories can be employed as soon as the distraction has been recognized. What counts as a substantial distraction can be illustrated with the example of meeting someone on the road, already mentioned above (see above p. 80). If such a meeting just leads to a brief greeting after which we move on, then it need not be considered a substantial distraction. But if we sit down to chat, then this would qualify as a substantial distraction.

In the case of substantial distractions, once we realize, we can look back and try to discern whether we have been experiencing lust, anger, or delusion, ideally also recognizing the feeling tone of that experience. Due to such mindful recognition, lust, anger, or delusion might just vanish. Nevertheless, for a short while we could still keep a lookout for a recurrence of these states. Such a lookout would be a way of recognizing their absence, and rejoicing in their absence will go a long way in preventing their recurrence.

If during practice we find the mind repeatedly getting into thoughts coloured by lust and anger, we might adjust to this situation by giving slightly more importance to impermanence in our main mode of practice. Awareness of impermanence, in particular in relation to pleasant and unpleasant feelings respectively, makes it easier to avoid reacting with desire and aversion. If our mind instead repeatedly gets into deluded distractions, we might give more importance to being fully alive to the present moment in our main mode of practice. In particular the subtle joy of being in the present moment prevents the type of boredom that often fuels the arising of distractions.

IMPERMANENCE

Sustained practice will make it unmistakeably clear that the mind constantly changes. A particular mental state arises only to pass away, followed by the arising of another mental state. Even that which knows is just a process. If it were permanent, it would forever be frozen in the condition of knowing a single thing. The very fact that the mind knows different things makes it indubitably clear that it cannot be permanent.

Any perception or thought is a messenger of impermanence, just as much as any feeling. Practising in this way fulfils the implications of clearly knowing (*sampajañña*). The canonical passage in question defines clearly knowing in terms of recognition of the impermanent nature of feelings, perceptions, and thoughts as they arise, persist, and then pass away (SN 47.35; Anālayo 2003: 39f).

The constantly changing nature of the mind becomes particularly evident when we get into the type of thought that we would rather avoid. Even though we sit down with the firm intention to cultivate what is wholesome, sooner or later we find that the mind has taken us for a ride and gone to a place where we certainly do not want to be. It becomes so patently obvious that we are not in control of our own mind. The mind is empty, just like the body.

Interestingly, those who have fully realized emptiness through full awakening are also those who have gained control over the mind. Controlling the mind is the result of skilfully working with the conditions of the mind through gradual training. It will not be achieved by merely trying to impose our willpower in the unreasonable expectation that the mind can just be forced to be the way we want.

Although we cannot force the mind to be the way we want, we are able to influence it by cultivating the appropriate causes and conditions. The realization of the conditioned nature of the mind undermines our sense of identification with our own thoughts, views, and opinions. On the positive side of this realization stands the insight that the way we are now is not an innate and unchangeable trait. Instead, it is the product of conditions. Conditions can be influenced and changed, and this is precisely where meditative training comes in. The conditions that are of crucial relevance in this respect are the topic of the fourth *satipaṭṭhāna*.

The insight perspectives that can be cultivated with contemplation of the mind complete our meditative appreciation of the three characteristics of impermanence, *dukkha*, and not-self. Body, feeling, and mind are without exception impermanent. What is impermanent is incapable of yielding lasting satisfaction. It is *dukkha*. According to the definition given in the first noble truth, one of the dimensions of *dukkha* is not getting what we want. This reflects our inability to control things completely. Body, feeling, and mind are clearly outside of the sphere of our complete control. For this reason, they have to be reckoned as devoid of a self. The self-notion targeted here is precisely about being in complete control. Therefore, what is impermanent and *dukkha* must be empty of a self.

The same understanding carries over from sitting to walking meditation. During actual walking, importance can be given to the constantly changing nature of the mind that is aware of the walking. Such observation can shift from awareness of impermanence to *dukkha* and eventually to the empty nature of all phenomena, whenever opportune. The comprehensive vision of body, feeling, and mind in their internal and external dimensions as being subject to the three characteristics reaches its completion at this point. Undertaken in this way, insight into the three characteristics can become our constant companion during any activity.

THE FOUR NOBLE TRUTHS

Insight into the three characteristics during any activity can take as its point of reference right view in the form of the four noble truths. With the previous *satipaṭṭhāna* practice this has already to some degree become a matter of personal experience. Having verified the practical relevance of this scheme of diagnosis, any problem or challenge in daily life can be approached with its help. This can take place by first of all honestly recognizing the stressful or even painful dimension of the problem or challenge (first truth), followed by discerning the degree to which our own attitude, expectation, or outlook makes a contribution to the stress or pain experienced (second truth). Such discernment in turn makes it quite clear that an adjustment on the side of our attitude, expectation, or outlook stands a good chance of diminishing, if not removing, the stress or pain (third truth). The medication to be applied (fourth truth) can then take the form of insight into the three characteristics. Whatever happens, it certainly is impermanent, therefore it is *dukkha* anyway, and most certainly it is empty of a self. According to what the situation demands, the medication could be by way of placing emphasis on one of the three characteristics or on all three in combination. The resultant right vision can have a substantially transformative effect, even to the extent of freeing the situation of its stressful or painful repercussions.

Such practical implementation of right view in turn builds a foundation for appreciating further dimensions of the noble eightfold path. Based on the directional input of right view and the compassionate dimension of right intention, it becomes unmistakeably clear why speech, action, and livelihood need to be brought into accord with this directional input. All of these need to evolve into becoming mindfulness-supportive behaviour. The mind is in a way comparable to a pot, which is easily overthrown if it has no stand. The stand required to steady the mind is precisely the noble eightfold path (SN 45.27).

The need for a firm moral foundation finds expression in several discourses in the *Satipaṭṭhāna-saṃyutta*. Each of these depicts how a monastic, who wants to go into retreat and do intensive practice, asks the Buddha for instructions. The instructions given emphasize the need to purify moral conduct (SN 47.3, SN 47.15, SN 47.16, SN 47.46, and SN 47.47). Established in purified moral conduct, the monastic should then cultivate *satipaṭṭhāna*. Another discourse even goes so far as to state that the Buddha's teaching of morality is precisely for the sake of the cultivation of the four *satipaṭṭhāna*s (SN 47.21). From an early Buddhist viewpoint, building a sound moral foundation is clearly indispensable for a proper cultivation of mindfulness.

THE DISTORTED PERCEPTIONS

The contribution made by contemplation of the mind to the hub of the wheel of practice is the knowing of the specific texture of the mind when mindfulness of the body is well established. In addition, at this point of practice insight into impermanence has become comprehensive, covering body, feeling, and mind. The body changes, that which feels the body changes, and that which knows body and feeling also changes. The contribution made to the rim of the wheel is a gradual lessening of identification with the mind. In this way the realization of emptiness also becomes comprehensive.

Looking back at the *satipaṭṭhāna* meditations cultivated up to this point, the first five spokes in the wheel involve a progressive cultivation of insight. This progress relates to the four distortions of perception (*vipallāsa*). These are the mistaken attributions of permanence, happiness, selfhood, and beauty to what in reality is otherwise (AN 4.49; Anālayo 2003: 25).

Contemplation of the anatomical parts undermines the mistaken projection of beauty onto the physical body. Practising with the elements deconstructs the erroneous assumption of a substantial self to be found anywhere in the body. This finds its complement in insight into the empty nature of the mind through the present exercise. Giving attention to our own mortality brings out the cutting edge of impermanence and thereby undermines the misleading assumption of any permanence in embodied existence. This also finds its complement in the present contemplation of mind, which makes it clear that the whole mental domain is also devoid of anything permanent. Contemplation of feeling brings out the true nature of felt experience. This directly counters the misguided attribution of happiness to what in truth and fact cannot yield lasting happiness: the pursuit of sensuality through the body. It does so by revealing a more promising arena for our innate quest for happiness: cultivating the mind in such a way that it becomes a source of wholesome joy and happiness.

A basic theme of the present *satipaṭṭhāna* is the importance of the mind regarding anything that happens. As the first verse in the *Dhammapada* proclaims, mind is the forerunner of dharmas (Dhp 1; Anālayo 2013: 145f). This role of the mind as the forerunner makes it all the more important that mindful monitoring of our mental condition be firmly established. The insight gained in this way leads to becoming increasingly adept at dwelling independently without clinging to anything.

SUMMARY

The main thrust of contemplation of the mind is towards an accurate reflection of the condition of our own mind, comparable to looking into a mirror. Instead of directing all attention to what happens outside, we learn to keep an eye on what happens within. Here the perhaps most important condition of the mind to be recognized and fostered is the presence of mindfulness. Such establishing of *sati* alerts us to the presence or absence of lust, anger, and delusion in the mind; it also enables our monitoring of deeper levels of concentration and insight. Ongoing practice reveals the impermanent nature of all mental events, including the quality of knowing itself.

VIII

HINDRANCES

With the sixth spoke in the wheel of practice presented here, we move into the domain of the fourth *satipaṭṭhāna*, contemplation of dharmas. In a way the fourth *satipaṭṭhāna* is a continuation of contemplation of the mind, by way of selecting specific mental states and factors: the hindrances and the awakening factors. In the mode of practice presented here, the three body contemplations under the first *satipaṭṭhāna* have their counterpart in three contemplations concerned with the mind, found under the third and fourth *satipaṭṭhāna*.

CONDITIONALITY

The distinct difference between the third and fourth *satipaṭṭhāna* is a direct working with conditionality. With the practice done so far, conditionality already came up with contemplation of the elements and contemplation of death, in the form of the realization of the dependency of the body on the elements, and in particular on a constant supply of oxygen, whose termination equals the ending of life. Conditionality then came to the forefront of attention with the second *satipaṭṭhāna*, by way of becoming directly aware of a crucial link in dependent arising: feeling as the condition for the arising of craving. Conditionality is also a significant undercurrent in contemplation of mental states, which soon enough makes it patently clear that we are not in control even in our own mind. Instead, the state of our mind is the product of causes and conditions, only some of which fall within the sphere of our direct influence.

With contemplation of dharmas an active exploration of conditionality is an explicit part of the instructions. What are the conditions that lead to the arising of the hindrances or the awakening factors? What are the conditions for overcoming the former and fostering the latter? Mindfully exploring these conditions is the central task of contemplation of dharmas.

The resultant thrust of these two contemplations of dharmas can in a way be seen as an exemplification of the famous dictum that one who sees dependent arising sees the Dharma and one who sees the Dharma sees dependent arising (MN 28; Anālayo 2003: 186). Directing our meditative seeing to conditionality comes in the present *satipaṭṭhāna* with a specific focus on those mental conditions that will lead to a state of mental balance in which the breakthrough to awakening can take place. Needless to say, the realization of Nibbāna is the converging point of all the teachings, the Dharma. Thus the combination of practically applied conditionality with the overall direction of progress to awakening seems to capture the gist of these two contemplations of dharmas.

Applied to situations outside of formal meditation, this gist can be actualized by taking into account whatever conditions present themselves in any situation and then relating these in one way or another to the liberating teachings. Although not every situation will be conducive to a cultivation of the awakening factors, there is hardly a situation or experience that cannot be considered from the viewpoint of the teachings. Reflections along the lines of, for example, "all things are impermanent" can provide just the input needed to ensure that the taste of the Dharma comes to pervade all of our experiences.

The actual instruction for contemplation of the first of the five hindrances proceeds as follows (MN 10):

> If sensual desire is present within, one knows: "sensual desire is present within me"; or if sensual desire is not present within, one knows: "sensual desire is not present within me"; and one knows how unarisen sensual desire arises, one knows how arisen

sensual desire is removed, and one knows how removed sensual desire does not arise in the future.

This type of instruction applies to each of the five hindrances, which are:

- sensual desire,
- anger,
- sloth-and-torpor,
- restlessness-and-worry,
- doubt.

Comparable to the two-stage procedure apparent in contemplation of feelings, contemplation of a hindrance also seems to proceed through two stages. The first stage is the recognition of the presence or absence of a hindrance in the mind. The second stage involves the distinct flavour of contemplation of dharmas in the form of a practical exploration of conditionality. Such exploration concerns the conditions that led to the arising of a particular hindrance, the conditions that can lead to its removal, and the conditions that can prevent its recurrence.

This two-stage procedure can conveniently be related to the fact that a hindrance can manifest in different degrees of strength. In the case of a weak occurrence of a hindrance, mindful recognition may be enough for it to disappear. In such a case, from a practical viewpoint we might just resume our main practice. After all, conditions for its arising must have been rather weak and the condition leading to its removal has clearly been mindfulness in itself.

At other times a hindrance can come up with greater strength. Becoming aware of it does not in itself suffice. This seems the appropriate situation for proceeding to the second stage of contemplation of the hindrances. In this way the presence of a hindrance in the mind can become a learning opportunity. The learning opportunity it affords concerns the conditionality of our own mind, in particular those conditions that led to the arising of the hindrance as well as those conditions most helpful for emerging from it and preventing its recurrence.

FACING A HINDRANCE

The type of attitude that I would recommend for this type of contemplation is similar to that of a good chess player. Imagine playing a game of chess with a good friend. Our friend has just made a threatening move, attacking our queen (*gardez!*). We will not get angry because of that. After all it is just a game and the other player is our good friend. Yet at the same time we do want to win.

With this type of attitude, wanting to win without getting angry, we examine the situation: "Let me see, how did I get into this? How come I am now in the situation of being about to lose my queen?" On examining how this happened, we keep a lookout for the type of move that will save our queen. In other words, we try to identify the condition that will lead us out of this situation.

For contemplation of the hindrances I recommend the same type of attitude. This involves almost an element of playfulness, combined with a strong intention to win the game. The more experienced we become with this type of game, the better chance we will have to win in the future, even to the extent of avoiding that our queen be put in danger in the first place. When viewed from this perspective, the occurrence of a hindrance becomes an occasion to train our skills, rather than a trigger for frustration and negative self-evaluation.

By cultivating such an attitude, we learn to take a hindrance less personally. The honest recognition that a hindrance is present does not mean that we have to own it and make it "mine". It can just be seen as something that has manifested in the mind, requiring appropriate action to be taken.

Taking a hindrance less personally not only eases possible tenseness of the mind when the presence of a hindrance is recognized, it also pays off in relation to its future recurrence. The degree to which this particular mental condition can actually function as a "hindrance", in the sense of obstructing our inner clarity, is inexorably interwoven with the degree of our identification with the images and associations it conjures up in the mind. The more we grow accustomed to no longer taking it personally, the better our chances that the next time it manifests we will be less easily caught up in the tendrils of identification. For this very reason we are more easily able to step back from believing in the conjured-up images and realize what is taking place.

Similar to the case of contemplation of mental states, it is helpful to explore the texture of the mind that is under the influence of a hindrance, to savour it distinctly and get a clear sense of its flavour.

As mentioned in the previous chapter on contemplation of the mind, when a hindrance is present our mind is neither great, nor concentrated, nor liberated. However, it is also surpassable, and learning how to surpass this obstructive condition will lead in the direction of the mind increasingly becoming greater, more concentrated, and more liberated. Whenever this happens, we can similarly explore the texture of the mind from which the hindrances are absent, to savour this condition distinctly and get a clear sense of its flavour.

Strictly speaking, actual removal of a hindrance is not a task of *satipaṭṭhāna*. Instead it belongs to the realm of right effort. As also mentioned in the previous chapter, for *satipaṭṭhāna* to lead to awakening it needs to be practised within the framework of the noble eightfold path. A discourse in the *Satipaṭṭhāna-saṃyutta* explicitly clarifies that the path leading to the cultivation of *satipaṭṭhāna* is the noble eightfold path (SN 47.40).

This noble eightfold path requires an initial appreciation of right view and the arousing of right intention, which leads on to building a foundation of moral conduct in its mental, verbal, and physical dimensions. Based on this foundation and a clear sense of direction by way of right view, right effort stands in its proper place, ready to assist when mere mindful contemplation is insufficient.

Needless to say, the employment of right effort does not stand on its own. It requires mindful monitoring in order to avoid both excess and deficiency in its deployment (Anālayo 2013: 183).

SENSUAL DESIRE

As already mentioned in an earlier chapter, the first hindrance of sensual desire (*kāmacchanda*) needs to be differentiated from desire as such (see above p. 51). Desire (*chanda*) can perform wholesome functions, such as the desire for liberation or for the welfare of others. The type of desire that is reckoned a hindrance is sensuality, the search for happiness through sex and sensual indulgence.

At times mindful recognition of the presence of sensual desire, or else an investigation of the causes that have led to its arising, can suffice to emerge from it. Should this not be the case and should we wish to respond to the occurrence of sensual desire by remaining within the framework of the *satipaṭṭhāna* meditation presented here, the next step could be to give emphasis to the impermanent nature of pleasant feelings. Pleasant feelings are bound to change; they do not last. Recognizing this will undermine the tendency to search for happiness through sensuality. Pleasant feelings are not only bound to change, but their disappearance will also sooner or later make room for the arising of painful feelings. To whatever degree we attach to the body during pursuits of sensuality, to that same degree we will be afflicted when pain manifests. Keeping in view this inherent danger helps to fortify our willingness to withstand the attraction of sensuality.

Should this still not suffice, we may bring in the standard antidote to the presence of sensual desire in the mind, which is to give attention to the lack of inherent attraction of what has triggered such desire (Anālayo 2003: 194 and 2013: 183). In the case of sexual desire this would be contemplation of the anatomical parts. Proceeding through the three body scans for skin, flesh, and bones will give the mind something to do and establish mindfulness of the body. Its main contribution, however, is to inculcate an attitude of non-attachment. Although this *satipaṭṭhāna* exercise is in particular about the notion of physical beauty leading to sexual attraction, it also arouses a general sense of non-attachment with all matters related to the body. This in turn undermines the basis on which the majority of our sensual desires thrive.

Other supporting conditions for dealing with the frequent occurrence of sensual desire are restraint of the senses and moderation with food (Anālayo 2003: 200). Both can in turn be undertaken as modes of cultivating mindfulness. Restraint of the senses has the same purpose as *satipaṭṭhāna* meditation, according to the part of the discourse that I like to refer to as the "definition". As mentioned in Chapter 2 (see p. 34), the definition relates *satipaṭṭhāna* meditation to dwelling free from desire and discontent with regard to the world. Similarly, restraint of the senses has the purpose of avoiding the arising of these two conditions. This confirms that, from a practical perspective, there is an overlap between *satipaṭṭhāna* and sense restraint (Anālayo 2003: 60).

When mindfulness is established at the sense-doors, it can exercise its protective function. Whether it be seeing, hearing, smelling, tasting, or touching, in each case mindfulness can alert us quickly when data comes in through a sense-door that stands a good chance of leading to detrimental repercussions in the mind. Restraint of the senses means cognizing the actual sense data without allowing further proliferations to occur. Such restraint of the senses can be supported by adopting a particular conduct, such as keeping the eyes downcast and living in seclusion. But it is not confined to such modes of behaviour. In fact, when moving out into the world, it will hardly be possible to maintain such a type of conduct.

Just trying to curtail sense experience will not be sufficient in itself, as can be seen in the *Indriyabhāvanā-sutta* (MN 152; Anālayo 2017c: 192). A brahmin student had proposed in front of the Buddha that the cultivation of the sense faculties involves not seeing and not hearing. The reply he received to this proposition was that, if this were the case, those who are blind and deaf should be reckoned accomplished practitioners. In other words, proper cultivation of sense restraint is not the mere avoidance of sense contact. Instead, it requires training in mindfulness. This can be supported by particular types of behaviour and by seclusion. These are means to an end, however, not ends in themselves.

Another way of forestalling the arising of sensual desire is to cultivate mindfulness with eating. The task is to remain aware that the purpose of food is to nourish the body, not to stimulate the taste buds. According to the *Brahmāyu-sutta*, when eating the Buddha experienced the taste of food without experiencing desire for the taste (MN 91; Anālayo 2017c: 202). The example set by the Buddha in this way can serve as an inspiration for cultivating mindful eating. In particular chewing properly before swallowing, so as to make sure the food is well masticated, can become a task for mindful monitoring. Doing so will increase health and at the same time counter the tendency to overeat (SN 3.13; Anālayo forthcoming a).

The potential of cultivating mindful eating and the insight that can arise from such practice is easily underestimated. According to a discourse in the *Saṃyutta-nikāya*, penetrative understanding of food can lead to going beyond sensual desire and thereby beyond further rebirth in the sensual realm (SN 12.63; Anālayo 2017c: 71). This goes to show that partaking of food can become a training ground for the cultivation of liberating insight.

One approach that can be helpful in this respect is mixing our food. In this form of practice, all the food is put into one bowl or container and then briefly stirred. This has the interesting effect that naturally sweet food items like raisins, for example, remain tasty. But artificial sweets like chocolate or cookies lose all their attraction on being mixed with soup, rice, and vegetables. The practice of mixing the food helps to let go of artificially sweetened food and find satisfaction with more natural and healthy food. In a very practical manner it brings home that the main task of eating is to nourish the body, rather than to entertain the taste buds.

For those wishing to take the same mode of practice a little further, there is the option of chewing our food and then, before swallowing it, taking it out of the mouth again for a brief moment of inspection. Another related dimension is the way the food looks when it leaves the body again as faeces and urine. Here an option would be to inspect both for a brief moment, sufficiently long to establish the connection in the mind between the visual and olfactory appearance the food eaten earlier has acquired by now and only then flush it down the toilet. In this way the whole picture of partaking of food is allowed to emerge before the watchful eye of investigation. This makes it easier to overcome a one-sided concern with its appearance before it enters the mouth and with its fleeting taste during the first few moments of chewing. Obsession with particular food is after all based on just these two fractional aspects of the entire process of feeding the body.

In addition, mindful investigation can also be applied to the experience of taste itself. Although the previously described approaches have already disclosed the degree to which the actual experience of taste corresponds only to a fraction of the whole process of food assimilation, closer inspection of this fraction further reveals the insubstantial nature of the experience of taste.

Slow eating with mindfulness soon enough shows that what the mind interprets as a seemingly continuous experience of pleasant taste in actual fact is a series of moments of tasting that are not invariably of the same degree of pleasantness. The realization dawns that, in the end, the degree of deliciousness of a particular meal is to a considerable extent a matter of mental projection. It is the mind that strings up moments of tasting, in combination with the anticipation evoked by visual and olfactory apperception, into the experience of a delectable meal. Appreciation of the contribution made in this way by the mind helps divest the attraction of taste of much of its ability to ensnare us with its deluding promise of true satisfaction through delicious flavours.

ANGER

The instructions for the hindrance of anger are:

> If anger is present within, one knows: "anger is present within me"; *or if anger is not present within, one knows: "anger is not present within me"; and one knows how unarisen anger arises, one knows how arisen anger is removed, and one knows how removed anger does not arise in the future.*

Here, again, mindful recognition or else investigation of what triggered the anger may at times suffice for it to go into abeyance. If this is not the case, we could direct attention to the impermanent nature of painful feelings. Whatever painful feelings there might be because of having been hurt or slighted by others, all such feelings are anyway bound to pass away. This understanding will diminish the subjective sense of a pressing need to take strong action on the external level against whoever has prompted our experience of painful feelings.

If contemplation of the impermanent nature of painful feeling is not sufficient to emerge from the arisen anger, the contemplation of the elements can offer additional help. Proceeding through the four body scans to discern earth, water, fire, and wind will keep the mind occupied and root mindfulness in the body, as well as arouse the perception of emptiness. Combining this with insight into the empty nature of the mind can go a long way in undermining the sense of a hurt ego that often nourishes anger. The same undermining of a sense of ego also helps to get out of the tendency to compare ourselves with others, resulting in subtle manifestations of anger in the form of competitiveness and envy.

The standard antidote to a tendency to anger is the cultivation of *mettā* (Anālayo 2003: 195 and 2013: 184). This reflects the opening of the heart mentioned in the previous chapter. In fact the *Sedaka-sutta* relates *mettā* to *satipaṭṭhāna* meditation, whereby we protect ourselves as well as others (SN 47.19; Anālayo 2003: 276, 2013: 244ff, and 2017a: 13ff). The cultivation of mindfulness and that of *mettā* share this quality of protection (Anālayo 2013: 24ff and 2015: 29f). The same nuance of protection through *mettā* is of relevance for external manifestations of anger. Mindful recognition that someone else is under the influence of this particular hindrance can naturally lead over to the appropriate response to this situation by way of cultivating *mettā*.

SLOTH-AND-TORPOR

The next two hindrances, sloth-and-torpor and restlessness-and-worry, are distinct in so far as both combine two mental conditions. The *Pariyāya-sutta* offers a mode of presentation according to which the five hindrances become ten (SN 46.52; Anālayo 2013:

186f). Here the first two hindrances can have an internal and an external dimension. The next two hindrances are divided into their individual parts. In other words, the third hindrance could involve either sloth or torpor; the fourth either restlessness or worry. It seems that in each case two mental conditions have been grouped together because their effect on the mind is similar. Here are the instructions for sloth-and-torpor:

> If sloth-and-torpor is present within, one knows: "sloth-and-torpor is present within me"; *or if sloth-and-torpor is not present within, one knows: "sloth-and-torpor is not present within me"; and one knows how unarisen sloth-and-torpor arises, one knows how arisen sloth-and-torpor is removed, and one knows how removed sloth-and-torpor does not arise in the future.*

In the case of the third hindrance, at times we may simply be tired and need to take a rest. Although there is a need to watch out for self-deception in this respect, there is a similar need to beware of being too hard on ourselves by denying the body rest when it really needs it. In the hot season the Buddha himself would at times take a rest during the day, when this seemed appropriate (Anālayo 2017c: 203). There is nothing intrinsically wrong with taking a nap when the body is too tired for meditation.

At other times, however, this particular hindrance may manifest as sluggishness or boredom. In other words, the present contemplation requires recognizing whether the tiredness is more of the body or more of the mind. We might also try to observe where the energy has gone, why it feels as if it has been used up, and how come it is at such a low level right now. At times, an undercurrent of anger can be discerned as what leads to sleepiness or drowsiness. At other times the cause could be avoidance, in the sense of not wanting to face things due to feeling overwhelmed. Another thing to check is our attitude towards the practice, which sometimes can lead to a lack of balance resulting in tiredness or a loss of inspiration. In general, rather than just fight this particular hindrance, we can try to understand its conditionality and, based on that, find creative ways to counter it.

A standard remedy for sloth-and-torpor is perception of *āloka*, a term which I take to mean mental "clarity" in this context rather than its literal meaning of "light" (Anālayo 2003: 197 and 2013: 184). On this interpretation, the task is to bring clarity into our meditation practice. A body scan with attention given to details of the anatomy would be a good example. At times meditating with eyes slightly open can also be helpful.

Brightening up the mind by recollecting a particularly inspiring teaching or by rejoicing in our virtues and meritorious deeds can also aid in overcoming this hindrance. In general, whatever arouses inspiration and energy is an appropriate means for emerging from this hindrance. In terms of the *satipaṭṭhāna* practice presented here, giving importance to the joy of being in the present moment can go a long way in arousing the type of joyful inspiration that directly counters boredom and sluggishness. If this should not suffice in itself, a potential remedy could be found in recollection of our own mortality, the third spoke in the wheel of practice. Giving attention to the inhalations with the understanding that this breath could be my last can stimulate the energy and effort that lead out of sloth-and-torpor.

For the case of torpor in particular, a discourse in the *Aṅguttara-nikāya* offers a series of remedies (AN 7.58; Anālayo 2003: 197). These are changing the meditation object, reflecting on or reciting the teachings, pulling the ears and massaging the body, getting up to sprinkle the eyes with water and looking at the sky, cultivating clarity of perception, and doing walking meditation. If these various methods should not have the desired effect, the time has come to lie down and take a rest.

RESTLESSNESS-AND-WORRY

The instructions for what in a way is the opposite type of hindrance, restlessness-and-worry, are:

> If restlessness-and-worry is present within, one knows: "restlessness-and-worry is present within me"; *or if restlessness-and-worry is not present within, one knows: "restlessness-and-worry*

is not present within me"; and one knows how unarisen restlessness-and-worry arises, one knows how arisen restlessness-and-worry is removed, and one knows how removed restlessness-and-worry does not arise in the future.

In the case of restlessness-and-worry, anything that calms the mind will be helpful. A useful tool here is again attention to the joy of being in the present moment, in particular with emphasis on resting in whole-body awareness. Relaxing into this joy will allow body and mind to become calm and tranquil, thereby directly opposing the tension and stress of restlessness-and-worry. The same type of practice will also help to emerge from the attitude of being too pushy and expending too much effort. Some degree of effort is indeed needed, but overdoing it will be detrimental to progress. It is important to cultivate contentment with our practice and its results. We meditate because this is simply the most meaningful thing to do, not because we desperately yearn for results. If goal-orientation can be left behind, meditation just progresses so much better.

A helpful example is the simile of a lute (AN 6.55; Anālayo 2003: 38), already mentioned briefly in Chapter 6 on the contemplation of feeling (see p. 114). If the strings are too tight, it will not be possible to play music. The same holds if the strings are too loose. Only when they are properly tuned is the lute ready for the performance. The same applies to the mind, which should be neither too tight nor too loose.

If the mind still remains agitated by restlessness-and-worry, we could rely on the third spoke in the wheel of practice by directing mindfulness to the breath, giving importance to the exhalations and to relaxing and letting go.

At times worries might manifest that actually need to be addressed. In such cases it is best to set aside the issue for the time being, promising ourselves that we will attend to it later. Here it is of crucial importance not to cheat ourselves. Once the meditation session is over, we should indeed attend to the worrying matter and think it over. Only if we keep our promise will the mind continue to be willing to set aside worrying matters during formal meditation on the next occasion.

DOUBT

The last hindrance is doubt:

> If doubt is present within, one knows: "doubt is present within me"; or if doubt is not present within, one knows: "doubt is not present within me"; and one knows how unarisen doubt arises, one knows how arisen doubt is removed, and one knows how removed doubt does not arise in the future.

Similar to the case of restlessness-and-worry, some types of doubt are best set aside when we are engaged in formal meditation, in order to be addressed later. This applies, for example, to fundamental types of doubt regarding the teachings. Here, too, we need to keep our own promise, in that once the meditation session is over the doubtful issue needs to be attended to with wise reflection.

Other types of doubt, however, can be concerned with how to proceed in our practice. There is an uncertainty about what to do with what has manifested and a wish for someone else with expertise to tell us. If a suitable guide is not available, we can at least try to become our own guide. This echoes the famous dictum that by practising *satipaṭṭhāna* we become self-reliant and an island to ourselves (SN 47.14; Anālayo 2013: 1).

Building up such self-reliance has its starting point in a mindful shift of perspective. Somewhat like flipping a coin over to the other side, we shift from the feeling of hopelessness to stirring up a keen sense of interest and investigation. In early Buddhist thought, the way to deal with doubt is investigation (Anālayo 2003: 199 and 2013: 207). Based on sufficient acquaintance with the teachings to serve the purpose of orientation, we investigate what is happening with mindfulness. We try out one possible solution. On finding that this does not work, we try out something else. Sooner or later something will work. In future we know how to deal with this situation, based on our own investigation and experience. We learn to trust ourselves and our ability as meditators. This is the fruit of our own investigation, based on having cultivated a clear distinction between what is wholesome or skilful (*kusala*) and what is unwholesome or unskilful (*akusala*).

Another dimension of doubt concerns our own abilities as well as the potential of the meditation practice we have adopted. Such doubt requires sustained investigation over a period of time. Not all meditation practices are equally suited for each practitioner. It follows that practice of a particular method is best monitored with mindfulness in order to see whether over time it yields results.

As mentioned in the previous chapter, the question here is less about getting into extraordinary experiences. Instead, the question is whether our ability to face difficulties and handle problems improves. Patience and understanding, as well as a gradual opening of the heart and a willingness to reach out to others, are important signposts. Finding that over longer periods of sustained and dedicated practice no significant result has manifested, it might be worth considering whether another meditation practice is perhaps better suited to our personality and needs.

Contemplation of the hindrances is not confined to the sitting posture. In fact the standard descriptions of walking meditation in the discourses speak of purifying the mind from obstructing states while sitting and walking (Anālayo 2003: 140). Thus recognizing (and overcoming) a hindrance can well take place during walking meditation or other activities.

THE ABSENCE OF THE HINDRANCES

Having investigated the presence of the hindrances and their conditionality, eventually there comes a time when no hindrance is present in the mind. Just as with contemplation of wholesome mental states, this is an occasion for arousing joy. Two sets of similes from the discourses are helpful in this respect.

One of these involves a bowl full of water used to see the reflection of our own face (SN 46.55; Anālayo 2003: 189 and 2013: 190f). A mind free from the hindrances has a crystal-clear quality just like pure water. Only pure water that is not mixed with dye, not heated up to the point of boiling, not overgrown with algae, not stirred by wind, and not muddied and placed in the dark will properly reflect the condition of the face.

The state of mental clarity that comes with the absence of the hindrances is similarly no longer coloured by the dye of sensual desire, which makes things appear quite differently from how they truly are. Such mental clarity is also not boiling with anger, which burns us and others. Nor is such a mind overgrown with the algae of sloth-and-torpor, resulting in stagnation. This type of mind is also not tossed around by the wind of restlessness-and-worry, resulting in a great deal of movement that does not lead anywhere. A mind like this is also not muddied and in the darkness of doubt, which prevents seeing reality as it is. Recollecting these vivid images can serve as an aid in recognizing the hindrances and in rejoicing in their absence.

The imagery of looking into a bowl of water to see the reflection of our face occurs not only in relation to the hindrances. As mentioned in the last chapter, the motif of looking into a mirror also describes contemplation of mental states (of others). The mirror imagery underscores the similarity between these two *satipaṭṭhāna* contemplations. Both require that we hold up the mirror of mindfulness. Inasmuch as such recognition is concerned, the task of mindfulness is to reflect clearly and accurately what is there, without reacting.

Just as a mirror shows up our external appearance the way it is usually only seen by others, in the same way the mirror of mindfulness provides us with an accurate reflection of our own mental condition, as if viewed from an uninvolved observation point. This inner mirror reveals to us the actual appearance of our mind which, due to our subjective investment in our own thoughts and ideas, is otherwise not so easily discerned. Yet it is only when a correct apperception of the actual state of affairs within has been gained, through looking into the mirror of mindfulness, that the proper foundation is laid for subsequently taking the appropriate action. This is why the third *satipaṭṭhāna* of contemplation of the mind is just about recognition as such. In the case of contemplation of the hindrances, the same mirroring function of mindfulness then probes further. As if magnifying the image reflected in the mirror, *sati* accurately reveals the conditions that have led to, and those that will lead out of, the particular hindrance whose presence the mirror within has disclosed.

The theme of absence of the hindrances is explicit in the second set of similes (DN 2; Anālayo 2003: 189 and 2013: 192f). Being free from sensual desire is like having settled a debt; both share a constant sense of being in need and wanting something. Recovering from anger is like recovering from a disease; in fact being angry is quite literally a form of dis-ease. Emerging from sloth-and-torpor as well as from restlessness-and-worry compare to being released from prison and slavery. Both predicaments involve a lack of personal freedom. Having safely crossed over doubt is like having safely crossed a dangerous desert. The time of exhaustion is over and safety has been reached. Emerging from all of these difficulties is indeed an occasion for rejoicing.

OPEN PRACTICE

Based on the foundation built by the first three *satipaṭṭhānas*, and imbued with the clarity of the mind that comes with the absence of the hindrances, we proceed to an unstructured mode of practice by way of open awareness. Firmly rooted in the strong post of mindfulness of the body we open up to the changing process of experience in whatever way it unfolds. Nothing can really disturb us, because whatever happens is food for mindfulness. In this way we continue progressing towards the final goal of a mind forever free from hindrances and defilements.

In terms of the simile of the wheel of practice, the contribution made by contemplation of the hindrances to the hub of this wheel is the mental clarity that accompanies our whole-body awareness. This is the mental clarity of being free from defilements, described in the series of similes related to a bowl of water. The contribution made to the rim comes to the fore in the other set of similes, according to which with the absence of the hindrances we are no longer in debt, diseased, imprisoned, enslaved, and in danger. This in turn facilitates dwelling independently, without clinging to anything.

SUMMARY

With contemplation of dharmas we embark on an active exploration of conditionality. Recognition of the presence of a hindrance in the mind leads on to examining what conditions have led to its arising and what conditions help us to emerge from it and prevent its recurrence.

Should we decide to respond to a hindrance from within the framework of *satipaṭṭhāna* meditation, then sensual desire could be countered by giving attention to the impermanent nature of pleasant feelings and with the help of contemplation of the anatomical parts; for the case of anger attending to the impermanent nature of painful feelings could be employed and contemplation of the elements.

The joy of being in the present moment can be of help if sloth-and-torpor or restlessness-and-worry manifest, by way of balancing out lack of energy just as much as its excess. Arousing inspiration and energy is the appropriate means for emerging from sloth-and-torpor in particular; an example would be attention given to the inhalations with the understanding that this breath could be my last. Giving attention to the exhalations combined with relaxing and letting go would then be an example for calming the mind as the appropriate means for emerging from restlessness-and-worry. The way to deal with doubt is investigation, either during actual practice or else subsequently.

The absence of the hindrances also deserves our attention. At such a time the mind has become clear like pure water that is not mixed with dye, not heated up to the point of boiling, not overgrown with algae, not stirred by wind, and not muddied and placed in the dark. Emerging from being overpowered by a hindrance is an occasion for joy, similar to having settled a debt, recovered from a disease, been released from prison and slavery, and having safely crossed a dangerous desert.

IX

AWAKENING

The last spoke in the wheel of *satipaṭṭhāna* practice presented here is contemplation of the awakening factors. The instructions in the *Satipaṭṭhāna-sutta* for the first of the awakening factors proceed as follows (MN 10):

> If the mindfulness awakening factor is present within, one knows: "the mindfulness awakening factor is present within me"; or if the mindfulness awakening factor is not present within, one knows: "the mindfulness awakening factor is not present within me"; and one knows how the unarisen mindfulness awakening factor arises, and one knows how the arisen mindfulness awakening factor is perfected by development.

This type of instruction applies to all seven awakening factors, which are:

- mindfulness,
- investigation-of-dharmas,
- energy,
- joy,
- tranquillity,
- concentration,
- equipoise.

Comparable to the two-stage procedure in contemplation of the hindrances, the present exercise also seems to involve two stages: the first stage requires recognition of the presence or absence of an awakening factor; the second stage then concerns exploring conditionality. This takes place by turning awareness to the conditions that lead to the arising of an awakening factor and those that will further strengthen it.

In actual practice, I suggest cultivating this first stage of recognizing the awakening factors based on the experience of joy due to the absence of the hindrances experienced with the previous contemplation. Such wholesome joy has manifested as a result of having become established in *mindfulness* as the all-important foundation and then having investigated the mind to check for the presence or absence of any of the five hindrances. This *investigation* has been carried out with sufficient *energy* to make sure the hindrances have indeed gone into abeyance. The *joy* that has arisen at such times naturally leads on to *tranquillity*, *concentration*, and *equipoise*. In this way, the build-up of practice achieved through the previous contemplation of the hindrances can be used as a launching pad for cultivating the awakening factors.

An important implication of the very presence of these seven awakening factors in our own mind is that it testifies to our capacity to awaken. However weak these awakening factors may be at present, through sustained cultivation they can be made to grow and become stronger. This in a way serves as a complement to our insight that body, feeling, and mind are empty, that they are not something we can truly own. At the same time, we do own something rather precious: the potential to awaken.

MINDFULNESS

Regarding the second stage in contemplation of the awakening factors, the main condition for the arising of the awakening factors is mindfulness itself. When *sati* is lost, the awakening factors lack their foundation. When mindfulness has been established, a sequential building up of the awakening factors can take place (Anālayo 2003: 235ff and 2013: 215ff).

Mindfulness as an awakening factor can be aroused through *satipaṭṭhāna* meditation itself (MN 118, SN 54.13, SN 54.14, SN

54.15, SN 54.16). The same can also happen, however, while listening to a talk (SN 46.3). A proper appreciation of this alternative requires a return to the topic of the relationship between mindfulness and memory, already broached in Chapter 1 (see p. 3ff). There I mentioned what seems to me to be a significant implication of this relationship for actual practice: mindfulness of what is present should be undertaken with the same kind of intent interest and open receptivity we would bring to anything that we are to remember later.

Imagine being given the task to witness a talk and later give an accurate report of it to others, but for some reason not being able to take notes and also not having access to anything that could be used for digital recording. Although such a scenario may seem somewhat remote nowadays, it does resemble quite closely the standard situation in the oral setting of ancient India. Thus to relate the awakening factor of mindfulness to the situation of listening to a talk would have been a natural way, in the Buddha's time, to illustrate the type of mental attitude and quality of the mind required in order to be able to remember later what was said.

Successfully remembering the talk and being able to give an accurate report to others would require that we arouse an attitude of keen interest and open receptivity while listening to it. We should do our best to avoid getting caught up in minor details and tangential associations. It would also be important to maintain a balanced attitude of unbiased observation rather than getting carried away by emotional reactions. Only in this way will we be able to ensure that we arrive at a balanced and comprehensive appraisal of the talk as a whole.

These qualities are precisely what *satipaṭṭhāna* meditation tries to inculcate: a keen interest, an open receptivity, as well as a balanced and unbiased observation. Here the two situations meet: the attempt to listen to a talk and remember it well, and the meditative cultivation of *satipaṭṭhāna*.

When the time has come to give our report of what we heard (or even when just wanting to recollect it for our own purposes), it would be helpful to establish a mental attitude as close as possible to the original situation of hearing. The more our state of mind resembles that of hearing the talk, the more comprehensive and precise will our recall of it be. This concords with the two dimensions of the contribution of mindfulness to facilitating memory: improved comprehensiveness and balance when storing information in the mind and ease of recall of that information later on. The same facilitation of taking in information and of its subsequent processing is a central dimension of the awakening factor of mindfulness during meditation practice.

A flavour of the awakening factor of mindfulness during actual practice could be summarized as its "sap", a summary based on combining the first letters of the following three qualities:

- soft,
- awake,
- presence.

Here "soft" is meant to represent the openness and receptivity that the mind acquires when *sati* is well established. This combines with an "awake" quality that comes about through following up the implications of the memory nuance of mindfulness, whereby we meet every moment with that inner wakefulness that will enable us to remember it vividly and distinctly. Based on a foundation in such inner wakefulness, mindfulness acquires its fully "awake" quality on being combined with the other awakening factors. The third quality of "presence" comes about when with mindfulness we remain fully in the present moment. In this way, the flavour of the "sap" of establishing mindfulness as an awakening factor could be summarized as a "soft awake presence". The combination of these three qualities can serve as a guide and reference point for knowing whether mindfulness is present (or absent) and for recognizing how *sati* arises and how to perfect it by development.

INVESTIGATION

Whether mindfulness has been established during a talk on the Dharma or with *satipaṭṭhāna* practice, the next awakening factor comes into being by examining, scrutinizing, and investigating the information that has become available through the open receptivity of mindfulness. The instructions in the *Satipaṭṭhāna-sutta* regarding the awakening factor of investigation-of-dharmas, *dhammavicaya*, are:

> If the investigation-of-dharmas awakening factor is present within, *one knows: "the investigation-of-dharmas awakening factor is present within me"; or if the investigation-of-dharmas awakening factor is not present within, one knows: "the investigation-of-dharmas awakening factor is not present within me"; and one knows how the unarisen investigation-of-dharmas awakening factor arises, and one knows how the arisen investigation-of-dharmas awakening factor is perfected by development.*

This particular awakening factor could be compared to using a magnifying glass. The rim that holds this magnifying glass is the teachings. These are the basic reference point for investigating whatever is happening in the present moment.

Such investigation-of-dharmas finds its expression in an attitude of keen interest, an inquisitiveness, a wish to follow things up and really understand them. An illustrative example would be the formulation used for contemplation of the elements in the *Ekottarika-āgama* parallel to the *Satipaṭṭhāna-sutta*. The instructions are: "In this body, is there the earth element, the water *element*, the fire *element*, and the wind element?"

Now there can hardly be any doubt that these four elements are found in the body. Hence I take it that the use of a question format conveys the type of attitude appropriate for investigation. The point at stake is to have an interested or even curious and inquisitive attitude, which does not necessarily have to be framed in words.

Following the lead provided by this example in the *Ekottarika-āgama* discourse, instead of just noting that things are impermanent, we might query: "Let me see, is this really changing? Is it indeed impermanent?" Holding this type of inquisitiveness as an attitude in mind, be it verbally or non-verbally, conveys a characteristic flavour of investigation-of-dharmas.

A particularly fruitful way of directing such an enquiring attitude during actual *satipaṭṭhāna* meditation is towards the condition of our own mind. This is precisely where the distinction made with the help of this awakening factor between what is skilful or wholesome (*kusala*) and what is unskilful or unwholesome (*akusala*) matters most. Investigating our own mind has an immediate benefit in so far as it supports the continuity of mindfulness, simply because any tendency towards distraction will more easily and more quickly be noticed. Such directing of investigation within can foster a form of meta-awareness that offers substantial support for *satipaṭṭhāna* meditation.

ENERGY

Establishing such an attitude of inquisitiveness within requires some persistence. A sustaining of investigation is needed in order for genuine progress to unfold. What sustains such investigation is the next awakening factor of energy, *viriya*. The instructions in the *Satipaṭṭhāna-sutta* on this awakening factor proceed as follows:

> If the energy awakening factor is present within, *one knows: "the energy awakening factor is present within me"; or if the energy awakening factor is not present within, one knows: "the energy awakening factor is not present within me"; and one knows how the unarisen energy awakening factor arises, and one knows how the arisen energy awakening factor is perfected by development.*

The energy mentioned in these instructions does not refer to the vital energy in the bodies of living beings. Instead, energy in the present context rather stands for persistence, in the sense of an active and continuous engagement with what we are doing and experiencing. According to the description given in the discourses that present the sequential building up of the awakening factors, such energy should be "unshaken" (*asallīna*). This confirms the importance of perseverance, of keeping with the task at hand, as a central nuance of energy as an awakening factor. Such active engagement can take on a bodily and a mental dimension.

JOY

The combination of being mindful, having an inquisitive attitude, and the sustaining support of active engagement leads up to a wholesome type of joy, *pīti*. The instructions in the *Satipaṭṭhāna-sutta* are:

> If the joy awakening factor is present within, *one knows: "the joy awakening factor is present within me"; or if the joy awakening factor is not present within, one knows: "the joy awakening factor is not present within me"; and one knows how the unarisen joy awakening factor arises, and one knows how the arisen joy awakening factor is perfected by development.*

The joy mentioned here relates to the subtle joy of being in the present moment, discussed in Chapter 6 on the contemplation of feeling (see above p. 114). It is this same subtle joy at a more mature and developed stage that can grow into the awakening factor of joy. The descriptions of the sequential building up of the awakening factors make it clear that such joy should be of an unworldly type. This circumscribes the kind of joy that can serve as an awakening factor. Rejoicing in the temporary absence of the hindrances from the mind would be a good example of a type of joy that fits the case.

Now the discourses regularly refer to a natural pattern where wholesome forms of joy lead on to tranquillity and concentration. This is the case to such an extent that there is no need to formulate an intention for wholesome joy to lead to tranquillity of body and mind, and for a tranquil body and mind to lead via inner happiness to concentration (AN 10.2; Anālayo 2003: 166). This in turn implies that an intentional arousing of the first awakening factors up to joy can build the foundation for a natural progression that sets in once joy is established, with only a need to monitor that this natural progression through tranquillity and concentration culminates in equipoise. Based on mindful investigation that is sustained by energy, the intentional arousing of joy seems to be a key factor in this whole sequential building up of the awakening factors.

TRANQUILLITY

The naturally soothing effect of wholesome joy leads on to tranquillity of the mind. The *Satipaṭṭhāna-sutta* instructs:

> If the tranquillity awakening factor is present within, *one knows: "the tranquillity awakening factor is present within me"; or if the tranquillity awakening factor is not present within, one knows: "the tranquillity awakening factor is not present within me"; and one knows how the unarisen tranquillity awakening factor arises, and one knows how the arisen tranquillity awakening factor is perfected by development.*

Tranquillity and calmness arisen in this way influence both body and mind. The body is at ease and the mind becomes calm. This becomes the manifestation of the awakening factor of tranquillity. According to the discourses that depict the sequential building up of the awakening factors, tranquillity of the body and mind leads to happiness (*sukha*), as a result of which concentration naturally arises.

CONCENTRATION

The instructions in the *Satipaṭṭhāna-sutta* regarding the awakening factor of concentration proceed as follows:

> If the concentration awakening factor is present within, *one knows: "the concentration awakening factor is present within me"; or if the concentration awakening factor is not present within, one knows: "the concentration awakening factor is not present within me"; and one knows how the unarisen concentration awakening factor arises, and one knows how the arisen concentration awakening factor is perfected by development.*

The standard translation of *samādhi* as "concentration" can at times call up unwarranted associations. However, since this is the generally established terminology, I think it is preferable for me in this case not to deviate from it and instead simply explain my understanding of the significance of the Pāli original. The term *samādhi* carries nuances of a bringing together (Anālayo 2003: 72). Such bringing together of the mind does not necessarily involve a narrow focus and certainly does not inevitably require the use of force, associations that can be called up by the term "concentration". Translations that perhaps better convey the nuances of *samādhi* would be "collectedness" or "composure" of the mind. All of this points to a condition of unruffled and unified serenity, which is the very opposite of being scattered and distracted.

From the viewpoint of the noble eightfold path, the concentration that arises at this point can fulfil the path factor of right concentration. A definition of this path factor speaks of the concentration that supports and is supported by the other path factors (MN 117; Anālayo 2003: 73). In fact, right concentration does not seem to be just a matter of reaching absorption attainment. The attainment of absorption could in principle be part of a form of practice that does not have the guiding principle of right view. Such concentration could not be reckoned "right concentration".

Absorption itself appears to have been already known in the ancient Indian setting before the time of the Buddha (Anālayo 2017a: 163ff). The distinct contribution by the Buddha seems to have been the perspective that such experiences are merely the product of specific conditions. This divests altered states of consciousness of any metaphysical or ontological connotations.

The Buddha's approach in this respect appears to have evolved from an analysis of absorption into three types to the more commonly found analysis into four types (Anālayo 2017c: 36ff). The existence of these two alternative schemes itself already shows that there is not just one possible mode of reckoning. What both schemes have in common is the analytical approach, the emphasis on conditionality. With the arising of such and such mental factors, such and such a type of concentrative experience can manifest. I take it that this perspective could be the backdrop of the often-found definition of right concentration by way of the detailed description of the four absorptions, reflecting the analytical approach and the vision of conditionality to be applied to these sublime experiences.

This in turn would imply that any level of concentration that has been reached, as long as this comes as part of a cultivation of the noble eightfold path and is approached with the same analytical attitude, deserves to be reckoned right concentration. In this way, differing definitions of right concentration found in the discourses could be reconciled with each other.

Here it would also be relevant that a discourse in the *Saṃyutta-nikāya* identifies the "stream" entered with the first level of awakening as being the eightfold path; hence one who is endowed with this path is called a "stream-enterer" (SN 55.5). This can hardly mean that every stream-enterer must be able to attain the four absorptions (Anālayo 2003: 79–81). Instead, a stream-enterer is accomplished in right view, and this would be what turns concentration, whatever its depth, into "right concentration".

EQUIPOISE

The culmination point in the cultivation of the awakening factors comes with equipoise, *upekkhā*, for which the *Satipaṭṭhāna-sutta* enjoins:

> If the equipoise awakening factor is present within, one knows: "the equipoise awakening factor is present within me"; or if the equipoise awakening factor is not present within, one knows: "the equipoise awakening factor is not present within me"; and one knows how the unarisen equipoise awakening factor arises, and one knows how the arisen equipoise awakening factor is perfected by development.

In other contexts, the term *upekkhā* stands for "equanimity". However, in the present context using that translation could be confusing, at least if this is understood to imply a contrast or even conflict with the existence of joy. This is not the case. In order to avoid possible misunderstanding, I prefer the translation "equipoise". In the context of the gradual building up of the awakening factors, *upekkhā* stands for a superb balance of the mind.

The Pāli description of the gradual building up of the awakening factors speaks of looking on well with equipoise at the concentrated mind. A Chinese parallel specifies that this refers to being free from covetousness and sadness (Anālayo 2013: 216). This relates back to the stipulation in the definition of the *Satipaṭṭhāna-sutta*, according to which we should dwell free from desires and discontent, or more literally covetousness and sadness. This correspondence conveys how the gradual building up of the awakening factors fruitions in what has been an aim throughout actual *satipaṭṭhāna* meditation: dwelling with inner balance (and returning to it as soon as it is lost).

A balanced cultivation of the seven awakening factors has as its starting point their sequential build-up, starting from mindfulness and culminating in equipoise. Such sequential building up of the awakening factors could be compared to playing a sitar with seven strings. Before beginning a piece of music, a player will first go once through the strings of the sitar one by one, from the lowest to the highest pitch. This is to make sure that they are properly tuned and in harmony with one another. No string should be too tight or too loose. After sounding each string in proper sequence, the sitar player is ready to perform.

Similarly, cultivation of the seven awakening factors can begin with a sequential build-up. Each of the awakening factors can be made to resound singly and in proper sequence. Once this has been done, the performance can start.

BALANCING THE AWAKENING FACTORS

The actual performance in the cultivation of the awakening factors is a matter of harmonious balancing. The basic tone that accompanies the entire piece is set by mindfulness. Mindfulness is always required (SN 46.53, Anālayo 2003: 235 and 2013: 204). The remaining six awakening factors fall into two ensembles with three members each. Investigation-of-dharmas, energy, and joy make up the members of the first ensemble, which serves to energize the practice. Tranquillity, concentration, and equipoise make up the members of the second ensemble, which serves to bring calmness to the practice. In actual practice, the concert pitch of these two ensembles could be summarized under the headings of "joyfully sustained interest" and "calmly composed balance".

Whereas the other six awakening factors need to be brought into balance, mindfulness is always required; it is their foundation and reference point. In a way, the other six almost seem to bring out nuances inherent in mindfulness by way of complementing and rounding off its awakening potential. The element of *inquisitiveness* naturally builds on the keen interest we bring to whatever we encounter through establishing receptive mindfulness, as if we had to remember it later. This element of inquisitiveness or sincere interest needs sustaining, it needs to be propped up with *energy* in the form of persistence. If this takes place without going overboard so as to result in tenseness, the *joy* of being in the present moment will saturate the resultant experience. In this way the three energizing awakening factors of investigation-of-dharmas, energy, and joy make their contribution in the form of a "joyfully sustained interest".

Alongside such joyfully sustained interest, well-established mindfulness has a natural dimension of *calming* body and mind. A mind with mindfulness established also tends towards *composure* rather than being scattered, and through *satipaṭṭhāna* practice the theme of balance and *equipoise* is very much in the foreground throughout. In this way the three calming awakening factors of tranquillity, concentration, and equipoise offer their contribution by way of a "calmly composed balance". In the company of these six, as ways of refining the inherent potential of *sati*, mindfulness fully acquires its marvellous awakening quality.

The *Aggi-sutta* illustrates the function of these two groups of three awakening factors with the example of a fire (SN 46.53; Anālayo 2003: 235 and 2013: 201ff). Wet material can be used to put a fire out, whereas adding dry firewood will make the fire flare up. The appropriateness of each type of material depends on the condition of the fire and what we want to do with it. If the fire is small and we want it to flare up, it is appropriate to add dry firewood and inappropriate to use wet material. The opposite holds for a big fire that we wish to reduce or put out.

The same applies for the cultivation of the awakening factors. Similar to the varying conditions of a fire, at times our mind might be slightly sluggish and at other times slightly excited. Noticing with mindfulness such minor fluctuations enables us to take the appropriate action. When the mind has become slightly sluggish, this is the time to give more emphasis to the first group of three. Giving emphasis to investigation-of-dharmas, energy, and joy will energize the mind and bring it back into balance. It would be unskilful at such times to give emphasis to the other three awakening factors that rather have a calming effect.

Conversely, when the mind has become slightly agitated or excited, it is time to strengthen the second group of three. Giving emphasis to tranquillity, concentration, and equipoise will calm the mind and bring it back into balance. In sum:

any mind: cultivate mindfulness,
sluggish mind: cultivate investigation, energy, joy,
agitated mind: cultivate tranquillity, concentration, equipoise.

In actual practice this could be illustrated with the example of being in a canoe or kayak with a double-bladed paddle. The canoe is carried forward by the flow of a river at exactly the right speed. On the banks to the left and right there is beautiful natural scenery and above is the wide-open sky. Our only task is to stay in the middle of the river so that the journey can continue on its own. This requires keeping an eye on deviating from the midst of the river. When the canoe moves closer to one of the two banks, gently putting one blade of the paddle into the water for a short moment suffices to return to the centre of the river.

In this simile, the canoe represents mindfulness of the body and the river the continuous awareness of impermanence. The beautiful scenery on both sides of the river illustrates the different insights to be gained during *satipaṭṭhāna* meditation. The wide-open sky represents the open-minded and receptive attitude characteristic of this mode of cultivating mindfulness. The ocean as the final destination of the river corresponds to the realization of Nibbāna.

One who cultivates the four *satipaṭṭhāna*s inclines and slopes towards Nibbāna just as the river Ganges inclines and slopes towards the ocean (SN 47.51). It is in particular the cultivation of the seven awakening factors that makes our practice flow towards Nibbāna (SN 46.77; Anālayo 2003: 233).

Returning to the canoe simile, the two blades of the paddle illustrate the emphasis to be given to one or the other of these two groups of three awakening factors. In order to continue the journey forward without getting stuck on the river banks, all that is needed is to keep an eye on remaining in the middle of the river, the midpoint of balance. Whenever the course of the journey begins to stray even slightly from that midpoint of balance, a brief use of one of the two blades of the paddle will bring about the necessary correction. This can happen either by placing more emphasis on the three awakening factors that energize or else by giving more importance to the three awakening factors that calm the mind. When well established, such balance can continue from sitting to imbue also walking meditation.

CULTIVATING INDIVIDUAL AWAKENING FACTORS

In addition to being grouped together into these two sets of three that are based on and interrelate with mindfulness, the awakening factors can also be cultivated individually. A discourse describes the degree of mastery that can be achieved in this respect (SN 46.4; Anālayo 2003: 240 and 2013: 205). Similar to a king or a minister who can freely choose whatever he wishes to wear from his full wardrobe, in the same way it is possible to learn to dwell in any awakening factor for however long we wish.

This passage encourages cultivating single awakening factors in order to gain familiarity with them and a clear understanding of each. Investigation-of-dharmas, for example, is clearly not confined to formal meditation. It can also be aroused through study and reflection on the teachings (SN 46.3; Anālayo 2003: 235). The same principle holds for other awakening factors. Their applicability to hearing or reflecting on the teachings would stand in the background of the recurrent reports of listeners attaining stages of awakening while the Buddha was delivering a discourse.

An applicability to situations outside of formal meditation would also be relevant to external contemplation, in the sense of noting whether someone else is mindful, for example, or has an investigative attitude, and so on.

Each of these seven awakening factors has its proper nourishment (SN 46.51; Anālayo 2003: 236 and 2013: 206ff). This provides yet another perspective on the conditions for arousing and stabilizing the awakening factors, the second stage in the instructions in the *Satipaṭṭhāna-sutta*. The nourishment for *mindfulness* is of course the practice of *satipaṭṭhāna* itself.

Investigation-of-dharmas finds its nourishment in clearly distinguishing between what is wholesome and what is unwholesome. Such clear distinction provides a crucial basis for *satipaṭṭhāna* meditation cultivated as an integral part of the noble eightfold path. It also provides a sense of direction for investigation, as the distinction between wholesome and unwholesome becomes naturally meaningful when observing the condition of our own mind. This is what above all needs to be constantly investigated and examined.

The awakening factor of *energy* has as its nourishment the making of an endeavour, which finds a prominent expression within the scheme of the noble eightfold path in right effort. The deployment of right effort is based on the ability to distinguish clearly between what is wholesome and unwholesome, a relationship that highlights the dependency of the awakening factor of energy on the preceding awakening factor of investigation-of-dharmas. In this way, by cultivating mindfulness and investigation we increasingly come to appreciate the distinction between what is wholesome and unwholesome, which in turn informs and directs the application of our effort and energy.

At this juncture of practice comes the experience of non-sensual types of *joy*. Giving attention to such joy (and those things that are a basis for it) is precisely what nourishes and establishes this awakening factor. I take this to imply, or even to sanction, the intentional arousing of wholesome forms of joy in order to proceed on the path to awakening. The next two awakening factors follow the natural course of events, where calmness of body and mind leads to *tranquillity* and in turn via non-distraction to mental composure in the form of *concentration* and eventually to *equipoise*. As already mentioned above, intentionally attending to joy sets the course that leads to the establishing of the remaining three awakening factors.

Another presentation helpful for appreciating practice-related dimensions of the awakening factors is the *Pariyāya-sutta*. The discourse depicts two possible domains for each of the seven, resulting in a total count of fourteen possible manifestations of the awakening factors (SN 46.52). Elsewhere I have discussed variations found in the Chinese parallel (Anālayo 2013: 209ff). In what follows I will rely on the Pāli version.

Mindfulness, investigation-of-dharmas, and equipoise can according to the *Pariyāya-sutta* have either an internal or an external dimension. In the case of mindfulness this is obvious, as the internal and external dimensions are explicitly mentioned in the refrain that comes after each individual contemplation in the *Satipaṭṭhāna-sutta*.

In addition to mindfulness, investigation-of-dharmas and equipoise can be directed to what is internal or else what is external. In other words, these three awakening factors appear to be particularly relevant for implementing this part of the refrain in the *Satipaṭṭhāna-sutta*. In this way, just as mindfulness can be cultivated internally and externally, so too investigation and equipoise can fruitfully be developed towards what happens internally and to what manifests externally.

An interesting aspect of the resultant grouping in the *Pariyāya-sutta* is that, whereas mindfulness is always required, investigation is an energizing factor and equipoise a factor that calms. From a practical perspective, I take this to imply that these two awakening factors can balance each other out. In other words, investigation-of-dharmas should not be taken so far that it results in a loss of equipoise. Conversely, equipoise should not inhibit the enquiry of investigation-of-dharmas.

A similar cross-relation obtains in the *Pariyāya-sutta* between energy and tranquillity. Both awakening factors can manifest bodily and mentally. In this way the external dimension is left behind and the description concerns just the internal dimension, which is further divided into the domain of the body and the domain of the mind. Here, too, an energizing factor and a calming factor stand in relation to each other. In terms of actual practice, I understand this to mean that, based on the balance established between investigation-of-dharmas and equipoise concerned with what is internal and external, in the realm of the internal a similar balance needs to be established between energy and tranquillity. In a way this is a natural interrelation, as too much energy will lead to a loss of tranquillity and excessive tranquillity inhibits the deployment of energy. Both situations equally lead to a loss of balance.

The remaining two awakening factors involve a further analysis of the domain of what is mental. Joy and concentration can be experienced at levels leading up to and including the first absorption and at deeper levels of absorption. The distinction drawn here involves the presence or absence of *vitakka* and *vicāra*, which as factors of absorption I understand to convey the sense of an application of the mind and its sustaining (Anālayo 2003: 75ff and 2017a: 123ff). In a wider sense, this distinction could also be understood to convey that joy and concentration can be aroused intentionally or else manifest spontaneously.

In the case of the awakening factors of joy and concentration, again a factor that energizes comes together with a factor that calms. Too much joy can become distracting and undermine the stability of concentration. Concentration taken up to a peak with the third and fourth absorptions leads to experiences where joy is left behind. For both to function as awakening factors, balance continues to be of central importance.

Based on the above presentation, the cultivation and balancing of the awakening factors could be visualized as involving three seesaws supported by a single pivot point. The single pivot point is mindfulness. The first seesaw has investigation-of-dharmas and equipoise as its two ends. It has the largest board because it encompasses the domain of what is internal and external. The second seesaw has energy and tranquillity as its two ends. Its board is comparatively smaller because it only covers the domain of what is bodily and mental. The third seesaw has joy and concentration as its two ends. Its board is the smallest because its domain is confined to various levels of deepening concentration.

Summing up, the cultivation of the awakening factors takes place based on a sequential building up. Mindfulness is the single pivot point for the three seesaws of investigation-of-dharmas and equipoise, energy and tranquillity, as well as joy and concentration.

INCLINING THE MIND TOWARDS AWAKENING

Progress to Nibbāna takes place by passing through four distinct yet interrelated meditative themes (Anālayo 2013: 219ff). The culmination point of these four meditative themes is letting go. Such *letting go* is reached via dwelling in dependence on *seclusion*, in dependence on *dispassion*, and in dependence on *cessation*. Just like the three legs of a tripod support its pinnacle, in the same way do seclusion, dispassion, and cessation support letting go. They invest letting go with the proper direction, in the sense that we need to let go of whatever is not in alignment with these three supports. Here seclusion can be understood to stand for having distanced ourselves from what is unwholesome (in particular the hindrances), dispassion can represent the fading away of attachments, and cessation can refer to the ending of *dukkha*. The final task then is to let go of what is unwholesome, what arouses passion, and what is *dukkha*.

A similar series of four meditative themes makes up the final tetrad of mindfulness of breathing in the *Ānāpānasati-sutta*, which is an alternative mode of cultivating contemplation of dharmas (MN 118; Anālayo 2003: 183). This final tetrad proceeds through the meditative themes of impermanence, dispassion, cessation, and letting go.

In relation to the mode of practice presented here, *satipaṭṭhāna* meditation undertaken so far establishes *seclusion* from the hindrances. During actual practice we keep an eye on this condition of seclusion, *viveka*, by maintaining mindfulness of the present moment without succumbing to distraction.

A secondary meaning of the term *viveka*, recognized in some dictionaries, is discrimination (Anālayo 2017a: 128). Although in its general use in the Pāli discourses the sense of seclusion is clearly the prominent one, this secondary meaning also has practical relevance. Once the mind is secluded from hindrances and distractions, we become able to discern the true nature of existence, in particular its nature of being subject to *impermanence*. This insight had in fact already become comprehensive with the previous three *satipaṭṭhāna*s. Seeing the changing nature of all aspects of experience naturally leads on to cultivating dispassion, to a gradual fading away of craving and attachments. Although this is a natural progression, it is nevertheless helpful to incline the mind intentionally towards dispassion. In a way, we are letting the implications of impermanence sink into the mind. We are allowing the flow of change to wash away our craving and attachments.

As our craving and attachments fade away through dispassion, we become increasingly able to be at peace with the ending of things; we are willing to allow things to cease. This serves to go beyond the average unbalanced attitude of only wanting what is young and new, ignoring what is old and decaying. By attending to the cessation of phenomena, to their ending, we arrive at a more balanced vision. It becomes more and more clear that cessation is not frightening, but actually peaceful. This becomes a practical implementation of insight into emptiness. As identifications lessen, it becomes increasingly easy to allow things to cease. This understanding spurs us onwards on the path to the supreme cessation of *dukkha*.

The more we are able to allow things to end, to be at ease with cessation and recognize its peacefulness, the better we will be at letting go. Gradually letting go of all remaining attachments prepares us for the supreme letting go, the plunge into the deathless, the realization of Nibbāna.

Needless to say, bringing these meditative themes into actual practice is not meant to encourage a tendency to fabricate experience. The proper use of these tools for progress in insight could be compared to a ray of the morning sun that touches a flower, causing it to open. The touch by the ray of the sun is like the skilful use of these themes; what follows is a natural development leading to the flowering of insight.

A simile in the *Saṃyutta-nikāya* describes a hen sitting on her eggs (SN 22.101; Anālayo 2003: 253). Due to her unrelenting sitting on the eggs, eventually the chicks will break the eggshells and hatch. In the same way, due to our unrelenting sitting on the meditation seat, eventually we will break the shell of ignorance and awakening will take place. It will occur in its own time. Our job is simply to make sure the appropriate conditions are in place. But the experience itself cannot be made or forced to happen. To try to do so would have the opposite result, as it would be directly contrary to what is most needed for awakening to take place: letting go.

In a way all of these meditative themes of seclusion, dispassion, cessation, and letting go point to Nibbāna. Each does so in a way that is a bit more pronounced or clearer than the previous one.

Proceeding through these meditative themes is quite different from a self-centred attempt to attain a certain experience. There is nothing to be acquired here. Rather, all and everything is to be let go of. Instead of reaching out to gain something, we allow the mind to resonate ever more strongly with the profound peace of Nibbāna. This is the peak of dwelling independently without clinging to anything in the world.

According to personal needs and preferences, we might move through these insight themes slowly or quickly. At times it may seem preferable to savour each distinctly. At other times it might feel appropriate to move more swiftly in order to give importance to their dynamic interrelation, leading up to the peak of letting go.

The basic dynamics involved in working through these four meditative themes could be visualized with the idea of a tiny slot between what is happening now and what happens next. Now our basic meditative task is to avoid being drawn into past and future. Instead, with mindfulness well established we learn to remain in the present. Once we are well established in the present moment, however, there remains a tendency of the mind to reach out for what comes next. This is like wanting to get the next spoonful of experience before having properly chewed the present one. By cultivating dispassion, we learn to let go of this reaching out for what is next and come to be at ease in just being with what is now. By moving on to cessation, the ending part of the present moment becomes fully clear to our meditative vision. Earlier this ending part was not properly noticed, due to the tendency to reach out for what comes next. As the ending of the present moment fully emerges, it becomes possible to let go into a tiny slot between what is now and what comes next. By letting go into that very slot, the breakthrough to Nibbāna can take place and timelessness can be experienced.

The *Satipaṭṭhāna-sutta* concludes by listing different time periods of practice leading to the two higher levels of awakening. Together with stressing the fact that *satipaṭṭhāna* is capable of leading to complete freedom of the mind from sensuality and aversion, this part of the discourse also offers the important indication that the time period to reach that goal can vary considerably.

The path to awakening involves a gradual progression, comparable to the gradual deepening of the ocean (AN 8.19; Anālayo 2003: 252). It is important to keep this in mind in order to counter unreasonable expectations of instant results and the consequent frustrations when these do not manifest. At the same time, however, some changes should manifest after sustained practice over a period of time. This is similar to a carpenter who notices that, after repeated use, the handle of his adze has worn out (SN 22.101; Anālayo 2003: 252). Repeated practice of *satipaṭṭhāna* should leave its marks on how we handle everyday situations. There should be small but noticeable changes for the better in our personal well-being and in how we relate to others.

OPEN PRACTICE

Returning to the actual practice, having aroused and balanced the seven awakening factors, we proceed to open awareness of changing phenomena in whatever way they manifest. We are aware that "there are dharmas" in terms of the awakening factors being established in balance, a balance that takes place in a mind that is firmly rooted in mindfulness of the whole body. Whenever the mind is established in seclusion, we can proceed via dispassion and cessation to letting go.

The contribution made by contemplation of the awakening factors in this way to the hub of the wheel of practice lies in establishing a superb mental equipoise and in imbuing the mind with the quality of being awake. The contribution made to the rim lies in particular in inclining the mind towards Nibbāna, the summit of dwelling independently without clinging to anything.

As for practice outside of formal sitting, at times a particular awakening factor can be aroused in specific situations when this seems opportune. Nevertheless, a cultivation of the whole set of seven is probably too subtle a form of practice to be easily applied in daily life. A helpful perspective for bringing essential dimensions of the present contemplation into ordinary situations can be found in a discourse that describes the factors that lead to the arising or origination of each of the four *satipaṭṭhāna*s (SN 47.42; Anālayo 2003: 106 and 2013: 175). In order to contextualize what this discourse has to offer for the fourth *satipaṭṭhāna*, I first briefly survey its presentation for the preceding three.

The discourse in question, the *Samudaya-sutta*, specifies the condition for the arising of the body to be nutriment. This dependency of the body on being nourished becomes quite evident with contemplation of the elements in particular, as discussed above (see p. 76). The body requires a constant supply of the earth element in the form of food (together with liquids, the appropriate temperature, and the necessary oxygen) in order to survive.

The *Samudaya-sutta* mentions contact as the condition for the arising of feeling. This highlights the conditionality of feeling, which is indeed the one *satipaṭṭhāna* that most easily lends itself to a direct and practical exploration of dependent arising at the crucial juncture where craving can arise. The impact of contact also underlies the distinction of feelings into bodily and mental types, which is precisely concerned with the type of contact that has led to their arising.

According to the *Samudaya-sutta*, the condition for the arising of the mind is name-and-form. This requires a bit of unpacking. My suggestion here is to read this part of the *Samudaya-sutta* alongside the way the early discourses list the first three of the four nutriments (*āhāra*). These are food, contact, and volition. The *Samudaya-sutta* lists food, contact, and name-and-form. So the first two items correspond in these two presentations; the third item is either volition or else name-and-form.

Now volition is one of the mental factors included in name. Based on this parallelism, I propose to interpret name-and-form in the context of the *Samudaya-sutta* as pointing particularly to the combination of mental processes and material impressions that set the context for and influence volition. By approaching name-and-form with a focus on volition in this way, a bridge to contemplation of the mind is more easily built. *Citta*, the word for mind, is etymologically related to *cetanā*, volition. A central task in contemplation of the mind is precisely to see through a particular train of thought and recognize the underlying current, the volitional driving force that stands behind it. Thus volition as a factor of name-and-form is indeed the condition for the arising of the mind. Just as food discloses the precariousness of bodily existence and contact the dependently arisen nature of feeling, in the same way a spotlight on volition captures an essential dimension of contemplation of the mind.

Turning to the fourth *satipaṭṭhāna*, according to the *Samudaya-sutta* attention (*manasikāra*) is the condition for the arising of dharmas. Similar to volition, attention is a factor of name and thus a quality present in any state of mind (unlike mindfulness). Just as volitions can be wholesome or unwholesome, a comparable distinction holds for attention. The basic quality of attention can be wise or penetrative, *yoniso*, or else it can be unwise or superficial, *ayoniso*.

From the viewpoint of contemplation of the hindrances and the awakening factors, the relationship established in the *Samudaya-sutta* between the fourth *satipaṭṭhāna* and attention acquires further significance. Attention is indeed crucial to both of these contemplations. Attention that is unwise or not penetrative, *ayoniso manasikāra*, leads to the arising of the hindrances and prevents the arising of the awakening factors, just as attention that is wise or penetrative, *yoniso manasikāra*, counters the hindrances and fosters the arising of the awakening factors (SN 46.24; Anālayo 2012: 199). In other words, the main thrust of the two contemplations of dharmas concerned with the hindrances and the awakening factors could be summarized in terms of cultivating *yoniso manasikāra*, wise or penetrative attention, over its opposite of unwise and superficial attention.

In this way, when viewed from a practical perspective, the presentation in the *Samudaya-sutta* can be interpreted as revealing a key point of contemplation of dharmas that can more easily be carried into everyday-life situations. This can take place through the simple contrast between wise or penetrative attention and its opposite. Directing our attention wisely or penetratingly is indeed amenable to any type of situation. It is also a form of practice that naturally builds a relation to the teachings, since it is precisely the input derived from acquaintance with the Dharma that supports the deployment of wise or thorough attention. The dimension of dependent arising also falls into place, since the thoroughness of vision that results from deploying wise or penetrative attention will sooner or later disclose the conditioned nature of whatever is experienced.

In sum, my suggestion is to bring contemplation of dharmas, in the way presented here as comprising the hindrances and awakening factors, into daily-life situations through the cultivation of wise or penetrative attention, *yoniso manasikāra*, in order to emerge from its opposite, *ayoniso manasikāra*.

Applied to all four *satipaṭṭhāna*s, the teaching of the *Samudaya-sutta* could then be interpreted to point to the four following aspects:

- become aware of the precariousness of bodily existence due to its dependency on *food*;
- explore the dependent arising of feelings at the point of *contact* (and learn to avoid reactions that increase *dukkha*);
- monitor *volition* in the context of *name-and-form* as that which sets the course of the mind;
- pay wise or penetrative *attention* to progress on the path to awakening.

SUMMARY

The task of the present contemplation is to recognize the presence (and absence) of the awakening factors as well as the conditions that arouse and stabilize each of these seven jewels in the mind. Based on *mindfulness* we *investigate* with *energy* such that *joy* arises, which naturally leads to *tranquillity* and *concentration*, culminating in a superb inner *equipoise*. Practice continues by maintaining a balance of these factors in the mind, comparable to a canoe in the middle of a river. Slight sluggishness can be countered by giving emphasis to the three energizing awakening factors, just as slight agitation can be balanced off through emphasis on the three calming awakening factors. Mindfulness is required throughout. With all awakening factors established in balance in a mind *secluded* from the hindrances, we cultivate *dispassion* and *cessation*, leading to ever deeper levels of *letting go*.

CONCLUSION

In this conclusion I summarize central features of the *satipaṭṭhāna* meditation I have presented in this book. Before doing so, however, I would like to make two disclaimers. My presentation in the foregoing pages does not come with any pretension on my side that *satipaṭṭhāna* in ancient India was undertaken exactly in the way I have described it here. Moreover, my descriptions and recommendations are by no means intended as the only acceptable way of putting into practice the instructions found in the *Satipaṭṭhāna-sutta* for progressing to awakening.

In addition to these two disclaimers, I would also like to put on record my indebtedness to the guidance I received when formerly practising in several Theravāda meditation traditions, in particular those taught by Ajahn Buddhadāsa, Mahāsi Sayādaw, and S.N. Goenka, without which I would not have arrived at the approach presented here. Perhaps even more significant is my indebtedness to Godwin Samararatne for having taught me the appropriate meditative attitude.

In the past I had the good fortune to encounter other practitioners who had attained levels of awakening. These were found among followers of several mainstream *vipassanā* traditions, such as those taught by Mahāsi Sayādaw, S.N. Goenka, and Pa Auk Sayādaw. Still others did not follow any particular tradition. I do not have any doubt that each of these *vipassanā* traditions is capable of leading to the breakthrough to stream-entry, just as I do not have the slightest doubt that what I present here has the same potential. Thus what I have described here is not meant to supersede other meditation traditions, but rather intended as offering yet another option for progress on the path. In short, my motivation is to enrich, not to compete.

Although the Pāli discourses are the framework and main orientation of my presentation, it should be clear that I have added my own ideas through bringing in such techniques as scanning the body. To my knowledge there is no textual basis in the early discourses for a body scan. Yet I found this particular practice helpful to make several contemplations in the *Satipaṭṭhāna-sutta* become more alive and accessible to direct experience. In this way, the preceding pages reflect my own personal approach for putting into practice what to my mind the early discourses convey.

In addition, I would also like to mention that what I am putting out here is done in the spirit of open-source. I point to the relevant passages and present my understanding as the result of my own practice and teaching experience in the hope of inspiring other practitioners to use whatever I offer to build their own practice, to become self-reliant.

BALANCE

In order to offer support and orientation for such self-reliance, in what follows I sketch a few central aspects of *satipaṭṭhāna* practice as described in the preceding pages. One of the central dimensions of *satipaṭṭhāna* meditation to be brought into being is balance. Now the first three exercises for body contemplation can be rather challenging. Contemplation of the body's anatomy aims at deconstructing the notion of bodily beauty, examining the elements undermines our identification with bodily existence, and recollection of mortality directly confronts what for most human beings is most fearful and dreaded: our own death. In the case of each of these practices, tools are readily at hand to establish and maintain balance in case this should get lost during practice.

If contemplation of the anatomical parts leads to a sense of aversion towards the body, we immediately shift to our good friend, mindfulness of the body, in order to re-establish balance. Through mindfulness of the body we learn to inhabit the body and be fully with it, such that it can become a foundation and reference point for the continuity of mindfulness.

Insight into the empty nature of the body by contemplating its elements has its natural counterpart in the opening of the heart to kindness and compassion. Should the absence of a self in bodily existence be experienced as a threat, emphasis on the opening of the heart and our interconnectedness with others and with outside nature can serve as a remedy. After all, what might seem in danger of being lost are just the narrow confines of a restricted and restricting sense of identity.

Facing our own mortality is probably the most challenging of the seven contemplations. Here the means to maintain balance are part of the very practice itself. Whereas attention given to the inhalations serves to bring home the truth of the precariousness of bodily existence, attending to the exhalations becomes a training in relaxing and letting go. Shifting the emphasis from one dimension of the process of breathing to the other enables us to maintain balance. As a whole, contemplation of death makes us become so much more alive to the present moment.

The three rather challenging body contemplations have their counterpart in three aspects of contemplation of the mind and of dharmas. The lessening of attachment that comes from insight into the absence of beauty in the physical body leads over to experiencing the beauty of the mind that is free from defilements.

The diminishing of our sense of ownership of the body, as a result of cultivating insight into its empty nature through contemplation of the elements, has its counterpart in the realization that we do own the potential to awaken. This becomes evident from the presence of the awakening factors in our own mind.

The courage to face our own death leads gradually to the point where, with letting go as the final of the four meditative themes to be cultivated with the awakening factors, we become ready for the plunge into the deathless. Both contemplation of the stages of decay of a corpse and the meditative themes to be cultivated with the awakening factors well established involve facing something challenging. Just as facing our own mortality leads over to becoming fully alive to the present moment, in the same way facing cessation leads over to the ability to let go into the experience of liberation.

The disconcerting discovery that the body is a constant source of subtle painful feelings has its counterbalance in giving attention to the subtle joy of being in the present moment. The recognition of mental defilements comes in conjunction with equal attention given to the joyful experience of temporary freedom of the mind. Finally, contemplation of the hindrances has its natural complement in contemplation of the awakening factors.

GRADUAL PROGRESSION

Another aspect of *satipaṭṭhāna* meditation is a gradual progression. This involves two dimensions. One of these concerns the meditative progression that results from implementing the stipulations of the refrain part of the *Satipaṭṭhāna-sutta*, the other involves the succession of the seven contemplations.

In line with the indications provided in the first part of the refrain, with any of the seven contemplations we at first explore aspects of each of the four *satipaṭṭhānas*. The double mention made of body, feelings, mind, and dharmas respectively is a feature common to the first part of the refrain and to each description of the individual contemplations. In line with this indication, we contemplate various anatomical parts, the elements, or the stages of decay in the case of the body. In relation to feelings and mental states we discern different types of each, and with contemplation of the hindrances and the awakening factors we proceed from their individual recognition to an exploration of their conditionality.

Moving from such internal practice during sitting meditation to walking or other activities, according to occasion and circumstances we round off our investigation of each of the four *satipaṭṭhānas* by attending to their corresponding external dimension. In the case of the first *satipaṭṭhāna*, the internal and external dimensions of the body are particularly accessible through the elements, although the same can of course also become evident with the anatomical parts and with recollection of death. With feelings and mental states, familiarity with their internal manifestations naturally leads over to recognizing their external counterparts when interacting with others. The same holds for the presence or absence of the hindrances and the awakening factors.

This exploration of individual aspects in their internal and external manifestations leads on to a comprehensive meditative vision of the impermanent nature of body, feelings, mental states, and dharmas, in line with the second part of the refrain. In the case of the first *satipaṭṭhāna* this is especially palpable with the changing nature of the breath as an exemplification of the impermanent nature of the body. This has become apparent already with the wind element and becomes fully evident with recollection of death. The same topic of impermanence continues seamlessly for feelings and the mind, as well as the hindrances and the awakening factors. Throughout, the focus of contemplation is no longer on an individual instance, be this a particular anatomical part, a specific feeling, or a certain state of mind. Instead, from the specific instance we proceed to a general appreciation of the impermanent nature of any manifestation of the contemplated phenomena.

The meditative progression that takes off from the individual contemplation in its internal and external manifestations, followed by discerning the nature of impermanence, leads over to the mode of practice of just being openly aware. During such open awareness the third aspect of the refrain moves to the foreground. From *doing* various contemplations we proceed to *being* mindful.

Being mindful of the whole body serves to know clearly that "there is the body", which forms the background to any of the three contemplations pertaining to the first *satipaṭṭhāna*. When with the second *satipaṭṭhāna* we begin noting the felt presence of the body, then this can serve for our awareness that "there is feeling" in relation to that very experience of being mindful of the body. The same can continue with the third *satipaṭṭhāna*, when we become aware of the knowing dimension of this same whole-body awareness in terms of "there is the mind". Moving on to the fourth *satipaṭṭhāna*, our continuous being aware of the whole body can then serve as the converging point for a balancing out of the awakening factors in the knowledge that "there are dharmas". In this way, awareness of the whole body can be a starting point for being mindful that "there is the body", "there is feeling", "there is the mind", and "there are dharmas", all done just for the sake of mindfulness and knowing.

Progressing through the four *satipaṭṭhānas* in the way presented here has not only brought out these different facets of the basic practice of awareness of the whole body, it at the same time has furnished complementary tools for maintaining this basic practice. Awareness of the whole body has received additional support through mindfulness of the breath as an easily discerned aspect of the body (to be cultivated without resulting in an exclusive focus on the breath that ignores the rest of the body). Another tool is the pleasant feeling of being in the present moment, which substantially empowers our ability to remain anchored in the here and now. Yet another aid comes from familiarity with the texture of our mind when it is with mindfulness. This familiarity helps to notice the early beginnings of a tendency to distraction through the resultant change in the texture of the mind, which in turn enables swift recovery before distraction has fully manifested. Building on these tools resulting from the progression through the first three *satipaṭṭhānas* in the way presented here, the cultivation of the awakening factors leads to a superb balance in the mind. This superb balance further fortifies our ability to put into practice the third part of the refrain by remaining mindful just for the sake of mindfulness and knowing. Whether, based on these tools, we are working with open awareness or else with any of the seven contemplations, throughout the task remains to dwell independently without clinging to anything.

Another gradual progression emerges with the seven

contemplations themselves. Here practice begins with the comparatively gross anatomical parts of the body. Next come the slightly subtler qualities of the elements in the body. The wind as the subtlest of these prominently manifests in the breath, which in the way of practice described here becomes a means for recollecting mortality. Further progressions from gross to subtle involve proceeding from the breath to that which feels the breath and the body, and then to that which knows feeling: the mind. Contemplation of mental states in turn leads on to the subtler exploration of conditionality in the mind. Here attention given to the conditions responsible for the comparatively gross hindrances leads over to becoming aware of the conditions for the subtler awakening factors.

Progressing in this way from gross to subtle has led to a gradual refinement of the hub of the wheel of practice I have been describing in this book: mindfulness of the body. The three body scans undertaken for contemplation of the anatomical parts have built up a foundation in rooting mindfulness in the body by progressively attending to skin, flesh, and bones, thereby proceeding from the body's external dimension to its internal parts. The same basic rooting of mindfulness in the body receives further strengthening with the four scans done for contemplation of the elements, which further refine whole-body awareness. With recollection of death, we become fully alive to the present moment and realize the importance of taking advantage of the precious possibility to practise right now, which substantially enlivens our dedication to the cultivation of mindfulness.

Building on this, contemplation of feelings enables the directly felt experience of change. This becomes further strengthened with contemplation of the mind, which contributes familiarity with the quality of mindful knowing as the facilitator of our direct experience of impermanence. Contemplation of the hindrances brings into being the element of mental clarity and contemplation of the awakening factors adds balance and the awake quality of the mind. In this way, the seven spokes of the wheel each make their contribution to a gradual building up of interrelated dimensions of the hub of this wheel.

The seven spokes of the wheel have also made their distinct contributions to its rim: dwelling independently without clinging to anything. The three body contemplations lead to emerging from obsession with bodily beauty, to a lessening of our identification with the body, and to facing the terror of our mortality. The second *satipaṭṭhāna* directly undermines the basis of clinging, which is craving arisen in dependence on feeling. The lack of control over the mind, so evident during practice of the third *satipaṭṭhāna*, brings about a lessening of our identification patterns and, in the mode of practice presented here, leads to a comprehensive insight into the three characteristics. Emerging from the hindrances empowers truly dwelling independently, and with the cultivation of the awakening factors we proceed to the peak of not clinging to anything by inclining the mind towards Nibbāna.

INSIGHT

Another important dimension of *satipaṭṭhāna* meditation is the cultivation of various types of insight. As mentioned in Chapter 1 (see p. 10), mindfulness on its own is not enough. However much the cowherd is continually mindful of the cows, he will not thereby progress to liberation. What he lacks is insight.

Progressing through the first three *satipaṭṭhānas* cultivates insights that directly confront the four distorted perversions (*vipallāsa*). Examining our anatomical constitution deconstructs the misleading projection of beauty onto the physical body. With the help of the elements and observation of mental states we counter the mistaken assumption of a substantial self to be found anywhere in the body or the mind. Facing our own mortality and contemplating the changing nature of feelings and mental states undermines the erroneous assumption of any permanency in our existence. Contemplation of feeling additionally brings to the fore of our attention the inherently unsatisfactory nature of all felt experience, weakening the misguided tendency to seek happiness where it cannot truly be found.

Three of the four distorted perversions concern the three characteristics of existence: impermanence, *dukkha*, and the absence of a self. These three characteristics stand in relationship to each other. Because what is impermanent cannot yield lasting satisfaction, therefore it is *dukkha*. Because what is *dukkha* fails to satisfy assumptions of complete control inherent in notions of selfhood, therefore it is empty of a self.

A firm foundation for this progression has been laid through facing our own mortality. This is the cutting edge of impermanence. Impermanence then becomes a directly felt experience with contemplation of feelings, which in turn reveals the inherently unsatisfactory nature of all that is felt. Proceeding to contemplation of the mind brings to completion the direct experience of the three characteristics by revealing the empty nature of the mind. In this way, these exercises from the first three *satipaṭṭhāna*s firmly establish the groundwork in insight into the three characteristics.

What remains to be done with the fourth *satipaṭṭhāna* is to proceed to the maturing point of insight, leading up to the breakthrough to awakening. This involves fine-tuning the mind through emerging from the hindrances and cultivating the awakening factors. With the awakening factors established, we proceed from the foundational theme of impermanence to its fruition in dispassion. Growing dispassion as an expression of our deepening appreciation of the truth of *dukkha* in turn enables us to see fully the disappearance aspect of what is impermanent, its cessation, which reflects a deepening realization of not-self. As we come to be at ease with cessation, we increasingly learn to let go, until eventually, as a sublime expression of the peak of letting go, we give up entirely all sense of ownership in relation to, or identification with, the empty phenomena of body, feeling, and mind.

As already briefly mentioned in Chapter 2, the meditative progression through the four *satipaṭṭhāna*s can be related to the four noble truths. In relation to the type of practice presented in this book, this would result in the following correlations:

Contemplation of the stages of decay of a corpse as a manifestation of our own mortality has put a spotlight on death, perhaps the most challenging manifestation of *dukkha*. This points to the first truth. Contemplation of feeling has made the arising of craving a matter of direct experience. This points to the second truth. Paying attention to a mental condition temporarily free from defilements gives us a foretaste of the final goal of total freedom from craving and attachment. This points to the third truth. Mindful recognition of the conditions responsible for the removal of the hindrances and the arousing of the awakening factors is a crucial ingredient for proper progress on the path to awakening. This implements the main principle underlying the fourth noble truth.

Spelled out in full, the fourth noble truth corresponds to the noble eightfold path. The first member of this path is right view, which in the discourses often takes the form of an appraisal of the four noble truths. This does not result in a tautology, but rather conveys that an initial appreciation of the four noble truths is necessary for setting out on the path of practice (Anālayo 2017c: 148f; see also Anālayo 2017a: 102ff). In fact a discourse in the *Saṃyutta-nikāya* explicitly states that right view is the precursor to a full comprehension of the four noble truths, just as the dawn is a precursor to the rising of the sun (SN 56.37). Dawn and sunrise differ in the degree of intensity of the sunlight. Similarly, an initial reflective acceptance of right view and the realization gained with full awakening differ in the degree of intensity of insight.

With contemplation of feeling, our initial appreciation of the four noble truths can become more a matter of direct experience. The experience of pain can lead to the understanding that the second arrow of mental anguish, a manifestation of *dukkha* that arises because of craving, can be avoided through mindful contemplation. Such direct experience of the viability of the diagnostic scheme of the four noble truths in actual practice can serve to confirm the accuracy of the guiding principle enshrined in right view.

The importance of right intention in turn can come to the forefront with contemplation of the mind, in particular in the dimension of intending to avoid harm, an expression of our compassion. The progress of insight through the first three *satipaṭṭhāna*s in turn makes it unmistakeably clear why mindfulness-supportive ethical behaviour is an indispensable requirement for genuine progress. This is what informs the implementation of the path factors of right speech, right action, and right livelihood. With contemplation of the hindrances, the foundation is laid for a proper deployment of right effort. The last path factor of right concentration then manifests fully with the arousing of the awakening factors. In this way, in the course of our practice it becomes plainly evident how the noble eightfold path serves as an indispensable framework for the type of *satipaṭṭhāna* practice presented here.

Besides actualizing the four noble truths and engendering the cultivation of the noble eightfold path, another closely related insight dimension cultivated with the practice discussed in the previous pages is dependent arising (*paṭicca samuppāda*). From a doctrinal perspective, dependent arising stands in close relationship to the four noble truths. Indeed the arising and cessation modes of dependent arising correspond to the second and third noble truths.

Contemplation of a corpse in its stages of decay, combined with recollection of our own mortality, has brought the final link in dependent arising to the forefront of our attention. With contemplation of feelings we turned to the crucial link where craving can arise. Through contemplation of the awakening factors we get ready for the breakthrough to the final goal of eradicating ignorance, the first link in the series. In each case, these central dimensions of dependent arising have shifted from the domain of intellectual understanding to becoming a matter of direct meditative experience.

DAILY-LIFE PRACTICE

Turning from the complexity of these various insight dimensions to simplicity, what remains as the hub of practice is mindfulness of the body. Whereas proceeding through the individual exercises is like a lotus with all petals open, daily practice requires that the petals be brought together.

In whatever situation we find ourselves, it is always possible to become aware of some part of the body as a starting point for arousing whole-body awareness. The sensation of feeling the body offers a door into recognizing the hedonic tone of present-moment experience, just as being aware of the presence of the body offers a point of access for becoming aware of the condition of our mind. Relating such practice of mindfulness to any form of insight ensures our progress on the path to liberation, the gist of the fourth *satipaṭṭhāna*.

This simple approach contains in a nutshell the significant contributions made by a form of practice that covers all four *satipaṭṭhāna*s. Here the first three *satipaṭṭhāna*s facilitate shining the light of mindfulness on the somatic, affective, and cognitive domains of experience, leading to their overall integration and alignment. This ensures that our appraisal of any situation, and our consequent reaction to it, takes into account each of these three domains. Based on this integration, the fourth domain completes the picture, by way of relating the whole situation in one way or another to conditionality and liberating insight.

If we wish to introduce just a little more complexity into this basic mode of practice of being aware of the body, giving emphasis to the skeleton in the body could be used to encapsulate the gist of the three body contemplations. Besides serving as a reminder of mortality, when the progressive decay of a body has reached the stage of a skeleton, all sexually attractive parts and markers of identity are gone. Attending to the skeleton within our own body can therefore be used as a reminder of all three dimensions of contemplation of the body.

In sum, all four *satipaṭṭhāna*s can coalesce into a single mode of practice that in principle can be undertaken in daily life. Such practice takes its nourishment from the more detailed modes of contemplation cultivated in formal meditation, when the lotus opens its petals. Their opening represents the flourishing of all four *satipaṭṭhāna*s in a continuous mode of practice.

ADJUSTING THE PRACTICE

This continuous mode of practice can be adjusted according to personal needs and requirements. If sensuality is a prominent issue, we might go through the anatomical parts in considerable detail and be less detailed with the elements. Facing our mortality could also take a prominent place, in order to bring home the fleeting nature of sensual indulgence. During contemplation of feelings we could be on the lookout for the impermanent nature of pleasant feeling in particular, and in relation to mental states we could check in particular for the presence or absence of a mind with lust. The first of the five hindrances and the conditions leading to its arising and passing away would naturally be prominent, and cultivation of the awakening factors could come with a special emphasis on dispassion.

If anger and irritation manifest frequently, after moving swiftly through the anatomical parts we might decide to go for a detailed and slow scan with the elements. Facing mortality would again have a contribution to make by way of fostering forgiveness. In the case of contemplation of feelings, the changing nature of painful feelings would offer a convenient point of emphasis, just as a mind with anger and the corresponding hindrance during the two ensuing contemplations. With the awakening factors, particular attention could be given to the theme of letting go.

If neither of these two cases described above fits our situation, chances are that the mode of practice appropriate for a tendency to delusion can fill the gap. In order to counter the basic mode of distraction that is so characteristic for deluded personalities, the first two body contemplations can help build up continuity of embodied mindfulness, followed by giving particular importance to coming fully alive to the present moment with contemplation of our own mortality. In addition, the joy of being in the present moment will help diminish the tendency to distraction. Neutral feelings and a deluded state of mind could become prominent aspects of contemplation of feelings and mental states. With the hindrances particular attention can be given to either sloth-and-torpor or restlessness-and-worry. Cultivating the awakening factors could be undertaken with a specific emphasis on the theme of cessation.

The above suggestions for working with the three basic character types are not meant to recommend a rigid scheme to be employed invariably in all sittings. Depending on how our meditation practice in general or even during a particular sitting unfolds, we might find that there is a need to adjust accordingly. Operating within the frame of the seven contemplations, at times the mind might just not be in the condition to arouse the awakening factors, for example. So we content ourselves with just establishing the first of these, mindfulness, and cultivate that much for the time being. Working with mindfulness is always helpful and on another occasion it might become possible to proceed to the other awakening factors.

The notion that we should find a single mode of practice and then stoically continue to pursue that mode for the remainder of our meditative life runs to some extent in a direction opposite to cultivating genuine mindfulness. Such genuine cultivation is very much about knowing what is happening right now and then adjusting practice in an appropriate manner, rather than going into autopilot mode as soon as we sit on the meditation seat.

A simile in the *Saṃyutta-nikāya* describes two cooks (SN 47.8; Anālayo 2013: 239). One takes no notice of the likings of his master. The other instead observes what his master likes, what type of food the master took most of or praised, and then adjusts his cooking to what he has observed. This is clearly the preferable way to proceed.

The foolish cook who just ignored how the food he prepared was received illustrates the case of a practitioner of *satipaṭṭhāna* who does not observe whether the practice undertaken leads to mental collectedness and to the diminishing of defilements. Clearly this is not the way to proceed. Instead, emulating the example of the good cook, it is our task to monitor with mindfulness the unfolding of our own *satipaṭṭhāna* practice. This requires paying attention to what type of practice suits us in general and also what is appropriate in the present situation.

In relation to the mode of practice I have presented in this book, this leaves open the door to adjusting the practice whenever opportune, even on a daily level if that seems required. My suggestion would be to maintain the framework of all seven exercises as a basic reference point and a marker of continuity. But within that framework each practitioner can place less or more emphasis on one or more out of these seven, and even give differing degrees of importance to particular aspects within a single contemplation.

For example, there could be a time when due to outer circumstances the topic of death naturally comes up. This makes it meaningful to give more room to the third spoke in the wheel of practice, to contemplation of a corpse combined with awareness of the possibly last breath so as to face mortality. Sometime later, something else might become more relevant and so we readjust. Introducing an element of creativity and inquisitiveness into the practice is helpful for swift progress to liberation.

KEY ASPECTS

The type of "attentiveness" to what the present situation requires, conveyed by the simile of the cook, together with the overall orientation towards "liberation" of *satipaṭṭhāna* as the direct path to the realization of Nibbāna, reflects two crucial qualities of the type of practice I have presented here. Together with another three key qualities, these converge on what I like to refer to in a condensed manner as the "pearl" of *satipaṭṭhāna* practice.

The first of these altogether five qualities finds expression in similes in the *Satipaṭṭhāna-saṃyutta* which describe how a monkey can avoid being caught by hunters and a quail can outdo a falcon as long as they stay on their respective home turf (SN 47.7 and SN 47.6; Anālayo 2003: 56 and 2013: 24ff). By remaining with mindfulness as our home turf we are "protected". The nuance of "protection" is also prominent in the simile of the two acrobats, mentioned in Chapter 2 (see above p. 37f). Both acrobats have to take care to protect themselves in order to be able to protect the other.

According to the mode of practice I have presented in this book, *satipaṭṭhāna* meditation can be implemented through cultivating an "embodied" form of mindfulness. Such mindfulness of the body finds illustration in two similes that describe six animals bound to a strong post and a person carrying a bowl brimful of oil through a crowd watching a beautiful girl dancing and singing, discussed in Chapter 1 (see above p. 19f).

Another quality also discussed in Chapter 1 is open "receptivity", exemplified by the simile of the cowherd who at the time when the crop has been harvested can just watch the cows from a relaxed distance (see above p. 9f). Adding to this the two aspects mentioned at the outset results in the following five qualities:

- protective,
- embodied,
- attentive,
- receptive,
- liberating.

Taking the first letter of each of these qualities leads me to the idea of the "p-e-a-r-l" of mindfulness meditation, as a way of summarizing what to my mind are key qualities of the *satipaṭṭhāna* practice I have presented here.

With this pearl of mindfulness established, we are "protected" during everyday life from the dire repercussions of unwholesomeness running its course unchecked. Such protection relies in particular on the cultivation of an "embodied" form of mindfulness as a rooting and reference point available in any situation. The mental space created in this way through mindfulness enables us to become much more "attentive" to what actually happens within and without, an ability that has its foundation in the open-minded broad "receptivity" of non-reactive mindfulness. On being combined with clearly knowing impermanence, such mindfulness propels our progress towards "liberation".

CULTIVATING TRANQUILLITY

In order to foster such progress towards liberation, *satipaṭṭhāna* meditation can be combined with the formal cultivation of tranquillity. As briefly mentioned in Chapter 1 (see p. 8), in early Buddhist thought tranquillity and insight are complementary dimensions of meditative cultivation. Hence there is no problem in allocating time for a practice like *mettā*, for example, alongside our *satipaṭṭhāna* meditation. A discourse in the *Satipaṭṭhāna-saṃyutta* explicitly recommends, in order to counter distraction or sluggishness, a temporary change from *satipaṭṭhāna* practice to tranquillity meditation (SN 47.10; Anālayo 2003: 64). Having in this way developed joy, tranquillity, happiness, and concentration, we are well equipped to return to *satipaṭṭhāna* practice.

A combination of tranquillity with our *satipaṭṭhāna* practice could be done by proceeding through the first six spokes in the wheel of practice, however quickly or slowly seems appropriate to the present situation. Based on the joy of seeing the mind free from the hindrances, we could next turn to cultivating tranquillity. Having dwelled for however long seems appropriate in tranquillity, we can move on to cultivating the awakening factors and progress through the awakening themes.

Cultivating tranquillity can in this way become an integral part of our meditative progress. Such integration has several benefits. One benefit is that it allows the growth of tranquillity alongside the cultivation of insight and thereby ensures that progress on the direct path takes place in a balanced manner. Meditation practised in this way stands much greater chances of leading to a successful transformation of personality for the better than monoculture of either tranquillity on its own or else dry insight by itself.

In the traditional setting, in the way it emerges from the early discourses, intensive meditation had its place based on a solid foundation in moral conduct and was part of a gradual process of training. This differs to some extent from the contemporary situation, where practitioners might come to join an intensive retreat without the necessary groundwork in place that can ensure balance of the mind. Here some cultivation of tranquillity can act as a buffer and facilitate progress in insight without loss of balance.

This is not to endorse meditation practice as a form of psychotherapy in its own right. Certain types of psychological problems are best addressed with the help of a therapist. If we have a backache, it does not make sense to go to see the dentist. The dentist is the right person to approach if we have toothache. Similarly, there are certain problems and issues that can and should be addressed in meditation. Other types of problems and issues, however, are best addressed with the professional assistance of those who have been trained in ways of dealing with them.

Nevertheless, as a complement to insight meditation practice, especially if this is carried out in an intense silent retreat setting, tranquillity has it place to ensure that our mental cultivation takes the form of a balanced development and indeed leads to dwelling independently, without clinging to anything. In this way, the cultivation of some degree of tranquillity recommends itself in several ways as an addition to *satipaṭṭhāna* meditation and as a way of empowering our progress on the path to liberation. In short, tranquillity deserves to become a supplement to the wheel of practice described in this book.

DWELLING INDEPENDENTLY

Whatever approach we might decide suits us best, be it the one described in the preceding chapters or one that has emerged from our own experience and needs, what counts in the end is the hub and rim of this wheel of practice. These provide the orientation point for gauging whether the mode of practice we have decided to adopt is moving in the right direction. Following this chapter, I present a succinct version of the wheel of practice, based on central aspects of each contemplation (see p. 218). In whatever way we might decide to engage in the seven contemplations, the gist remains throughout that we become increasingly well established in mindfulness of the body during formal meditation as well as daily activities, this being the hub of the wheel, and that practice results in our ability to dwell independently without clinging to anything, corresponding to the rim of the wheel.

SUMMARY

A key aspect of *satipaṭṭhāna* meditation is balance. If contemplation of the anatomical parts should lead to a loss of balance by way of negativity towards the body, this can be countered by emphasis on embodied mindfulness as our good friend. If the empty nature of body and mind should become too challenging, turning to the opening of the heart and our interconnectedness with nature outside can be of help. Facing our mortality with the inhalations has its natural counterbalance in relaxing and letting go with the exhalations. Similarly, the discovery that the body is a constant source of pain has its counterbalance in the discovery of the subtle joy of being with mindfulness established in the present moment.

Moreover, the deconstruction of bodily beauty with the first exercise has its natural counterpart in the discovery of mental beauty in a mind temporarily free from defilements. Lack of ownership over body and mind leads up to the discovery that we own the ability to awaken. Having faced death, we proceed with our *satipaṭṭhāna* meditation until eventually, with the cultivation of the awakening factors, we draw close to the realization of the deathless.

In the mode of practice presented here, awareness of the whole body serves as a reference point throughout. This can be further enhanced by including the process of breathing as an aspect of this experience of the whole body. Another tool for maintaining momentum of practice is the joy of being in the present moment and familiarity with the texture of the mind when mindfulness is present.

In terms of the simile of the wheel of practice, the hub of this wheel has received support from the first two body contemplations by way of rooting mindfulness in the body and from recollection of death by way of making us come fully alive to the present moment. The second *satipaṭṭhāna* contributes to this the felt sense of change and the third *satipaṭṭhāna* familiarity with the texture of the mindful mind. The absence of the hindrances adds to this mental clarity and the awakening factors provide a superb balance and awake quality of the mind.

The rim of the wheel has received similar support. The three body contemplations have established non-attachment, a lessening of our sense of identification with the body, and the ability to face our mortality. Through insight into the impermanent nature of feelings we keep directly undermining craving and, based on the third *satipaṭṭhāna*, we have arrived at a comprehensive insight into the three characteristics. Building on the overcoming of the hindrances, we cultivate and balance the awakening factors such that we indeed dwell independently, without clinging to anything.

The four *satipaṭṭhānas* can coalesce into a single mode of practice that in principle can be undertaken in any situation during everyday life, as long as we establish whole-body awareness. Based on such grounding in bodily reality, we can become aware of the repercussions of what is happening on the feeling and mental level, and in some way arouse insight, such as, for example, by noting the impermanent nature of what is taking place. In this way daily-life experiences and formal meditation can enhance each other and in conjunction lead to balanced and sustained progress along the direct path to realization.

THE WHEEL OF SATIPAṬṬHĀNA PRACTICE

THE HUB: embodied mindfulness

THE SEVEN SPOKES:

Contemplation of

the body:	1) anatomical parts: skin, flesh, bones	}	non-attachment (optional: not beautiful / not sexually attractive)
	2) elements: earth, water, fire, wind	}	empty of a self
	3) mortality: skeleton and this in-breath could be the last	}	impermanence
feelings:	4) pleasant, unpleasant, neutral	}	impermanence and conditionality
mind:	5) mindful / not mindful; in addition: lust / no lust, anger / no anger, delusion/ no delusion	}	impermanence, therefore *dukkha*, therefore empty
dharmas:	6) hindrances: sensual desire	antidotes:	impermanence of pleasant feelings, anatomical parts
	anger	antidotes:	impermanence of unpleasant feelings, emptiness
	sloth-and-torpor	antidotes:	joy of present moment, inhalation as last breath
	restlessness-and-worry	antidotes:	joy of present moment, relax and let go on exhalation
	doubt	antidote:	investigation
	7) awakening factors: mindfulness	=	foundation
	investigation, energy, joy	=	energizing
	tranquillity, concentration, equipoise	=	calming

progression of insight: seclusion – dispassion – cessation } letting go

THE RIM: dwelling independently without clinging to anything

QUOTATIONS

In what follows I provide references to the standard English translations of the passages quoted in the course of my exploration (except for quotes from MN 10, which are from my own translation in Anālayo 2013: 253ff), in order to enable the reader to follow up any of these and consider them in their original context.

EPIGRAPH

SN 47.15 (p. xv)   Bodhi 2000: 1645

CHAPTER I   MINDFULNESS

SN 47.5 (p. 5)	Bodhi 2000: 1631
AN 1.6.1 (p. 6)	Bodhi 2012: 97 (reckoned as no. 52)
DN 15 (p. 8)	Walshe 1987: 226
MN 19 (p. 9)	Ñāṇamoli 1995/2005: 209
MN 38 (p. 11)	Ñāṇamoli 1995/2005: 360
SN 47.9 (p. 19)	Bodhi 2000: 1637
SN 47.14 (p. 19)	Bodhi 2000: 1645
SN 35.206 (p. 20)	Bodhi 2000: 1255 (reckoned as no. 247)
SN 47.20 (p. 20)	Bodhi 2000: 1649
MN 119 (p. 21)	Ñāṇamoli 1995/2005: 954
AN 8.19 (p. 22)	Bodhi 2012: 1144
SN 45.4 (p. 22)	Bodhi 2000: 1526
MN 119 (p. 22)	Ñāṇamoli 1995/2005: 955

CHAPTER II   *SATIPAṬṬHĀNA*

MN 118 (p. 25)	Ñāṇamoli 1995/2005: 943
SN 47.4 (p. 27)	Bodhi 2000: 1630

CHAPTER VII   MIND

DN 2 (p. 132)	Walshe 1987: 106
MN 5 (p. 133)	Ñāṇamoli 1995/2005: 108
MN 51 (p. 135)	Ñāṇamoli 1995/2005: 450
MN 19 (p. 143)	Ñāṇamoli 1995/2005: 208
SN 47.35 (p. 146)	Bodhi 2000: 1657
SN 45.27 (p. 148)	Bodhi 2000: 1537
SN 47.3 (p. 148)	Bodhi 2000: 1629
SN 47.15 (p. 148)	Bodhi 2000: 1645
SN 47.16 (p. 148)	Bodhi 2000: 1646
SN 47.46 (p. 148)	Bodhi 2000: 1662
SN 47.47 (p. 148)	Bodhi 2000: 1663
SN 47.21 (p. 148)	Bodhi 2000: 1650
AN 4.49 (p. 149)	Bodhi 2012: 437
Dhp 1 (p. 149)	Norman 1997/2004: 1

CHAPTER VIII   HINDRANCES

MN 28 (p. 152)	Ñāṇamoli 1995/2005: 283
SN 47.40 (p. 155)	Bodhi 2000: 1660
MN 152 (p. 157)	Ñāṇamoli 1995/2005: 1147
MN 91 (p. 158)	Ñāṇamoli 1995/2005: 747
SN 3.13 (p. 158)	Bodhi 2000: 176
SN 12.63 (p. 158)	Bodhi 2000: 598
SN 47.19 (p. 160)	Bodhi 2000: 1648
SN 46.52 (p. 160)	Bodhi 2000: 1603
AN 7.58 (p. 162)	Bodhi 2012: 1060 (reckoned as no. 61)
AN 6.55 (p. 163)	Bodhi 2012: 933
SN 47.14 (p. 164)	Bodhi 2000: 1645
SN 46.55 (p. 165)	Bodhi 2000: 1611
DN 2 (p. 167)	Walshe 1987: 101

CHAPTER IX   AWAKENING

MN 118 (p. 172)	Ñāṇamoli 1995/2005: 946
SN 54.13 (p. 172)	Bodhi 2000: 1782
SN 54.14 (p. 172)	Bodhi 2000: 1785
SN 54.15 (p. 172)	Bodhi 2000: 1786
SN 54.16 (p. 172)	Bodhi 2000: 1786
SN 46.3 (p. 173)	Bodhi 2000: 1571
AN 10.2 (p. 177)	Bodhi 2012: 1340
MN 117 (p. 179)	Ñāṇamoli 1995/2005: 934
SN 55.5 (p. 180)	Bodhi 2000: 1793
SN 46.53 (p. 181)	Bodhi 2000: 1607
SN 46.53 (p. 182)	Bodhi 2000: 1605
SN 47.51 (p. 183)	Bodhi 2000: 1665
SN 46.77 (p. 183)	Bodhi 2000: 1622
SN 46.4 (p. 185)	Bodhi 2000: 1573
SN 46.3 (p. 185)	Bodhi 2000: 1571
SN 46.51 (p. 185)	Bodhi 2000: 1598

CONCLUSION

ABBREVIATIONS

AN	*Aṅguttara-nikāya*
Dhp	*Dhammapada*
DN	*Dīgha-nikāya*
MN	*Majjhima-nikāya*
SN	*Saṃyutta-nikāya*
Vibh	*Vibhaṅga*

REFERENCES

Anālayo, Bhikkhu 2003: *Satipaṭṭhāna, The Direct Path to Realization*, Birmingham: Windhorse Publications.

— 2012: *Excursions into the Thought-world of the Pāli Discourses*, Washington: Pariyatti.

— 2013: *Perspectives on Satipaṭṭhāna*, Cambridge: Windhorse Publications.

— 2014a: "Exploring Satipaṭṭhāna in Study and Practice", *Canadian Journal of Buddhist Studies*, 10: 73–95.

— 2014b: "The Mass Suicide of Monks in Discourse and Vinaya Literature", *Journal of the Oxford Centre for Buddhist Studies*, 7: 11–55.

— 2015: *Compassion and Emptiness in Early Buddhist Meditation*, Cambridge: Windhorse Publication.

— 2016: *Mindfully Facing Disease and Death, Compassionate Advice from Early Buddhist Texts*, Cambridge: Windhorse Publications.

— 2017a: *Early Buddhist Meditation Studies*, Barre: Barre Center for Buddhist Studies.

— 2017b: "The Luminous Mind in Theravāda and Dharmaguptaka Discourses", *Journal of the Oxford Centre for Buddhist Studies*, 13: 9–49.

— 2017c: *A Meditator's Life of the Buddha, Based on the Early Discourses*, Cambridge: Windhorse Publications.

— 2018a: "The Bāhiya Instruction and Bare Awareness", *Indian International Journal of Buddhist Studies*, 19: 1-19.

— 2018b: "Once Again on Mindfulness and Memory", *Mindfulness*, 79: 1–6.

— 2018c: *Rebirth in Early Buddhism and Current Research*, Boston: Wisdom Publications.

— forthcoming a: "Binge Eating and Mindfulness in Ancient India".

— forthcoming b: *Mindfulness of Breathing, A Practice Guide and Translations*.

Bodhi, Bhikkhu 2000: *The Connected Discourses of the Buddha, A New Translation of the Saṃyutta Nikāya*, Boston: Wisdom Publications.

— 2012: *The Numerical Discourses of the Buddha, A Translation of the Aṅguttara Nikāya*, Boston: Wisdom Publications.

Ñāṇamoli, Bhikkhu 1995/2005: *The Middle Length Discourses of the Buddha, A Translation of the Majjhima Nikāya*, Bhikkhu Bodhi (ed.), Boston: Wisdom Publications.

Norman, K.R. 1997/2004: *The Word of the Doctrine (Dhammapada)*, Oxford: Pali Text Society.

Thiṭṭila, P.A. 1969: *The Book of Analysis (Vibhaṅga), The Second Book of the Abhidhammapiṭaka, Translated from the Pāḷi of the Burmese Chaṭṭasaṅgīti Edition*, London: Pali Text Society.

Walshe, Maurice 1987: *Thus Have I Heard; The Long Discourses of the Buddha*, London: Wisdom Publications.

INDEX

WINDHORSE PUBLICATIONS

Windhorse Publications is a Buddhist charitable company based in the UK. We place great emphasis on producing books of high quality that are accessible and relevant to those interested in Buddhism at whatever level. We are the main publisher of the works of Sangharakshita, the founder of the Triratna Buddhist Order and Community. Our books draw on the whole range of the Buddhist tradition, including translations of traditional texts, commentaries, books that make links with contemporary culture and ways of life, biographies of Buddhists, and works on meditation.

As a not-for-profit enterprise, we ensure that all surplus income is invested in new books and improved production methods, to better communicate Buddhism in the 21st century. We welcome donations to help us continue our work – to find out more, go to windhorsepublications.com.

The Windhorse is a mythical animal that flies over the earth carrying on its back three precious jewels, bringing these invaluable gifts to all humanity: the Buddha (the 'awakened one'), his teaching, and the community of all his followers.

Windhorse Publications	Perseus Distribution	Windhorse Books
info@windhorsepublications.com	210 American Drive	PO Box 574
	Jackson	Newtown
	TN 38301	NSW 2042
	USA	Australia

THE TRIRATNA BUDDHIST COMMUNITY

Windhorse Publications is a part of the Triratna Buddhist Community, an international movement with centres in Europe, India, North and South America and Australasia. At these centres, members of the Triratna Buddhist Order offer classes in meditation and Buddhism. Activities of the Triratna Community also include retreat centres, residential spiritual communities, ethical Right Livelihood businesses, and the Karuna Trust, a UK fundraising charity that supports social welfare projects in the slums and villages of India.

Through these and other activities, Triratna is developing a unique approach to Buddhism, not simply as a philosophy and a set of techniques, but as a creatively directed way of life for all people living in the conditions of the modern world.

If you would like more information about Triratna please visit thebuddhistcentre.com or write to:

London Buddhist Centre	Aryaloka	Sydney Buddhist Centre
51 Roman Road	14 Heartwood Circle	24 Enmore Road
London E2 0HU	Newmarket	Sydney
UK	NH 03857	NSW 2042
	USA	Australia

Mindfully Facing Disease and Death: compassionate advice from early Buddhist texts
Bhikkhu Anālayo

This unique anthology from the Buddha's early discourses focuses on guidance for facing disease and death, and has the overarching theme of *anukampā*: compassion as the underlying motivation in altruistic action.

The author draws on his own translations from the Chinese *Āgama* collection, presented here for the first time, alongside their counterparts from the Pāli texts, enabling readers to compare the parallel versions in English translation. Taken together with Anālayo's practical commentary we gain a first-hand impression of what early Buddhism had to say about disease and death.

These teachings invite us to integrate their guidance directly into the laboratory of our own meditation practice and life, in the spirit of deep investigation and inquiry. As committed meditation practitioners know first hand, there is no more worthy or meaningful introspective undertaking in the world, nor a more difficult challenge for human beings to adopt and sustain throughout life. – From the Foreword, Jon Kabat-Zinn

An invaluable and extraordinary resource on the profound teachings by the Buddha on dying, death, and grieving. Bhikkhu Anālayo has given a great gift to all of us by bringing together in this book the compassionate wisdom of the Buddha on our mortality. – Roshi Joan Halifax

This is an indispensable book for serious students of Buddhism. It has the potential to transform the lives of everyone who reads it. – Toni Bernhard

I believe the Buddha would rejoice in this book and exhort all of us to read it and apply the medicine within. This will help to bring about the deepest healing of all – the healing of the mind and the heart – even if we are slipping over the final frontier of death itself. – Vidyamala Burch

ISBN 978 1 909314 72 6
£13.99 / $19.95 / €16.95
320 pages

ALSO BY BHIKKHU ANĀLAYO

A Meditator's Life of the Buddha: based on the early discourses
Bhikkhu Anālayo

The author offers an inspiring biography of the Buddha based on the early discourses. By focusing on his meditative development and practice – on the Buddha as a meditator – Anālayo seeks to provide inspiration and guidance to all meditators, of any tradition and any level of experience. Each of the twenty-four chapters concludes with suggestions to support meditative practice.

While offering a scholarly portrait of the Buddha, this book is also a testament to the overarching unity of the various early Buddhist schools in their conception of the Buddha's life, a unity that coexists along with a rich diversity in their detailed narrations about particular events in that life. – Bhikkhu Bodhi, scholar and translator

An inspiring guide that will accelerate the reader's own journey of awakening. Highly recommended, and sure to inspire dedicated meditators! – Shaila Catherine, author of *Focused and Fearless: A Meditator's Guide to States of Deep Joy, Calm, and Clarity*

The extremely useful exercises with which each chapter concludes ground the scholarship in a fervent awareness of the goal, represented by the Buddha, which we should always have in mind in our own practice. – Jinananda, author of *Warrior of Peace: The Life of the Buddha*

Anālayo's mastery of both the Pāli and the Chinese sources, as well as the scholarship that surrounds them, makes him an unrivalled authority, and an attentive guide to the Buddha's explorations of the mind and meditative states. – Vishvapani, author of *Gautama Buddha: The Life and Teachings of the Awakened One*

ISBN 978 1 909314 99 3
£13.99 / $19.95 / €16.95
280 pages